for Wi[illegible] gratitude, And Love.
Tony

We are all on our own unique paths, albeit from the same place, to the same place. But the truth is that we don't have to make an effort at anything, except to get out of our own way by clearing our mind of our judgments.

To be available to hear new voices and to be open to new ideas, the more we will broaden our consciousness. – Sri Mokki

Please get well And feel great.

Other Books by Tony Seton

Covid Blue
Thought So
True Tens / Seven Women of Beautiful Character
Truth Be Told
Mayhem
Jennifer
The Francie LeVillard Mysteries - Volumes I- XI
The Francie LeVillard Mysteries - The Early Years
Just Imagine
Trinidad Head Say It Write
The Flight of KAL 007
The Bright Wise Solution
Mokki's Peak
Is There a Why?
Selected Writings
Deki-san
Equinox
Silent Alarm
No Soap, Radio
Paradise Pond
Selected Writings
The Autobiography of John Dough, Gigolo
Silver Lining
The Omega Crystal/New Moves
13 Days of Fear
Musings on Sherlock Holmes
The Brink
Dead as a Doorbell
The Quality Interview / Getting it Right
on Both Sides of the Mic
From Terror to Triumph /
The Herma Smith Curtis Story
Don't Mess with the Press / How to Write,
Produce, and Report Quality Television News
Right Car, Right Price

The Ultimate App

It's free, it's pre-loaded, and it runs your life

The Ultimate App

It's free, it's pre-loaded, and it runs your life

by Tony Seton

September 2022

Pebble Beach, California

This is not a work of fiction. It's reporting on a number of significant personal experiences and conversations, plus research in the work of such fine minds as Carl Jung, Abraham Maslow, Robert A. Johnson, George Leonard, Wendy Palmer, Shirley Luthman, and others.

The Ultimate App

It's free, it's pre-loaded, and it runs your life

ISBN: 978-1-7375932-2-5

Printed in the United States of America

Thank You

To the good people who have contributed to my life, particularly those who shared their love and wisdom ... this book is for you.

And a special note of appreciation to Jules Hart for proofing the book.

Table of Contents

The Ultimate App

1 - Introduction

A house is no home unless it contains food and fire for the mind as well as the body.
– Margaret Fuller

I started collecting information for this book several years ago because I was fascinated by some of my experiences dealing with how the mind works, and seriously interested in attaining greater awareness and higher consciousness. What I have learned is exciting and too important not to share.

In these pages I have reported what I've seen and learned, to put before you ideas that might echo what you have seen, heard about, and felt yourselves. Some of what you read here could validate your own experiences, feelings, and thoughts, and be something of a platform for you to expand your awareness and move forward to a higher level of consciousness and a more rewarding life.

Also, it might be an impetus for you to share what you know with others, because if what I have learned is widespread, as it might well be, it could be that we are on the verge of an evolutionary transformation that could turn out to be more significant than the fish climbing out of the water.

I say that with all humility, and recognition of a growing interest in synchronicity. And a surge in consciousness that is coming at a time of growing violence and political reversion...what a coincidence!

The more you learn about your mind and how it works, the more impressed you will be about what it can do for you. The more you are open to what it can do for you, the more you will benefit from it. Understand that your mind is not physical; it has no form. Your mind is energy, only energy. It is where your thoughts and feelings live, not in your brain. It is your non-physical heart. It operates 24/7, from the time of your conception until you pass. Its sole purpose is to make your life the best you can be.

Some notes ...

- We will start off with an explanation of the basics of us as human beings, especially what our mind is in our lives.

- When I reference a person as an example, it will be he/him/his for the most part, rather than switching or using s/he. It's not sexist, it's to save time and space.

- There is some repetition because different subjects

need the same references.

- Much of the book reports on what and from whom I have learned about the mind. I don't suggest that it should be your experience. I'm just providing a context that may facilitate your understanding.

- Toward the end there is a section of *Bits and Pieces* that are relevant, relatively quick to understand, and didn't need their own chapter.

At the end of the book you will find *Thoughts of Sri Mokki*. It is a collection of guidelines from *Mokki's Peak*, a novel I wrote 25 years ago, in which a wise man generously shares his wisdom with a hungry soul.

You might choose to skip to the end to see what Mokki is all about, and then return to the beginning to find out "the rest of the story", that is, how I got here from there and what else I discovered that will be of interest and significant to you.

2 - The Ultimate App

Do what you can, with what you have, where you are. – Theodore Roosevelt

First, the title. *The Ultimate App* is the human mind, so the subtitle – *It's free, it's pre-loaded, and runs your life* – should make sense because it plays an omniscient role in the way you live your life, from beginning to end.

You didn't have to pay for the app or install it because it's been with you since your conception. Your precognitive life was managed by your human equivalent of your computer's ROM (Read-Only Memory) that mostly ran your physical being alone for the first six months or so, until your mind could become more involved.

The ROM continues to operate the body's primary physical functions, but it is your mind – *The Ultimate App* – that makes the decisions that run your life as you know it.

This book explains how your mind operates and

your involvement in the process. You actually know everything that you will read in these pages, but that information has been pushed out of easy mental reach. You pushed it to the back of your mind when you were learning from your parents and others around you in your earliest years. They were teaching you how to communicate and then what they thought you needed to know as you grew up.

That wisdom that you were born with, that was pushed aside as you were being clued in to how life worked, was what Carl Jung called the *collective unconscious*. That includes all the information that was recorded from the memory and experience of all our ancestors. Jung said that the same information is available to all human beings, and it is accessible to people if they understand its existence. It can also be found if they are in a crisis state.

3 - The Factors

Man is so made that he can only find relaxation from one kind of labor by taking up another.
- Anatole France

Here is a quick introduction to the primary players:

Your Mind - Your mind is not your brain. Your brain is physical. Think of your brain as hardware and your mind as software. Your mind operates in conjunction with your brain. Your brain receives information from throughout your body and from outside of it through the five senses - taste, touch, sight, sound, and smell - and that information is interpreted by your mind. Your mind also manages information that comes to you in the form of thoughts and feelings from your True Self. Your mind also picks up information from external sources including people, places, and things, both known to you and not, both near and far.

Your True Self - Your True Self is your being - who you are - often referred to as your soul. It is the pure energy that started you off, matching the right sperm to the appropriate egg that became the physical you. The True Self is a nexus to everyone and everything in your life. Every bit of information that comes from the True Self to your mind is true. Your True Self experiences feelings and thoughts without any overlay. Your True Self speaks the truth without a mask. The departure of your True Self from your physical being marks your passing.

Your Intuition - Your intuition is the voice of your True Self. It comes to your mind as a thought.

Your Instinct - Your Instinct carries non-verbal messaging from the True Self as feelings.

Your Ego - Your Ego is a personality in your mind that you create as an interface to deal with people, places, and events outside of yourself. Your Ego may vary from the True Self's unvarnished truth when it perceives that it is necessary to communicate with others for reasons of safety, manipulation, generosity of feelings, and other purposes. Note that the variance from the truth of the True Self may be reasoned, e.g., to avoid danger or unnecessary damage to you or others, out of courtesy, and in the exercise of humor or instruction.

Your Universe - Your universe is everyone and everything that you are aware of or otherwise perceive through your senses, thoughts, feelings, and dreams. Everyone's universe is unique.

4 - Getting Started

The supreme accomplishment is to blur the line between work and play. – Arnold J. Toynbee

While you started at conception, you are not really operating for six months or so. Your main distinguishing components are the physical and mental DNA of the two principle contributors, usually your parents. Another critical factor in your first stage is the environment in which those six months have been spent. The physical and the emotional conditions of the mother, in particular, but also outside influences including other people, events, and circumstances in which your early life existed.

It was long thought that infants took their first breath in the world as *tabula rasa.* It was philosopher John Locke's term for the brand-new human mind, which he wrote in 1689 was a blank slate. That's not widely accepted anymore. Considering the parental factors that defined the sperm and the egg, and the environment in which the fetus was grown, it is implausible that the new being is coming into the light unmarked.

Most of us come into life as good, healthy beings; undamaged during the fetal journey by a physical misadventure or an environment of anger, fear, danger, or the woman not wanting to be a mother. And when we are born, we arrive with a sense of participation, responsibility, and obligation. This is critical to the health of the planet.

> Not every fetus has such a positive experience. Those who wind up being adopted often have serious emotional, behavioral and/or health issues. These children have as many as problems as non-adoptive children, and more still than children of biological parents who are together. This can hardly be a surprise, considering that an adoptive child is produced in the body of a woman who doesn't want it or knows she can't keep it, in an environment that can't be supportive of the infant in the womb. This is not to suggest that abortion should be encouraged. Rather, that sex education should be required for all teens, and the subject of adoption should be fully explained as a regrettable alternative. Further, it strongly suggests that we should buy off those people who would not be good parents from having children.

* * * * *

Like in computers, the ROM gets the body newly

outside of the womb and into the world up and running with new essential operating instructions. Those instructions are so vital to your survival that they are read-only so you can't mess with them. Your ROM has your heart beating, your blood flowing, your lungs breathing, your brain calculating, and your senses operating at a basic level. With all these mechanical devices working, it's unimaginable to think that your mind arrives empty.

Carrying forward the comparable computer functions, your personal early mental activity is functioning like the RAM (the Random Access Memory) which is your unique programable mental workspace ... your Mind. At some point during the pregnancy, it becomes operational. It takes in information and sorts it in some manner, maybe to be saved, discarded, used, edited, replaced, or temporarily forgotten.

5 - Moving Forward

A bit beyond perception's reach I sometimes believe I see that life is two locked boxes each containing the other's key. – Piet Hein

After your birth, you are immediately on a path of your own in negotiating your world. You have to figure out the stimuli that come your way, both from inside - hunger, discomfort, fatigue, confusion, pain, soothing - and from outside, i.e., the physical environment and the people on your stage. For a while it's probably something of a blur, and then you begin to be able to identify and classify your experiences.

In a healthy situation, you will be dealing with loving parents who see to your needs and instigate basic communications with you. That's important, of course, but there is an inherent problem in this "natural" progression from zygote to adult, and that is that the parents, with all good intentions, teach you much of what they were taught at your age by their parents, who got much of their basics from your great-grandparents, going back at least in some cases many generations.

Consider first that you are in a supportive environment, soaking up a detailed description of, and instructions about, how life works. What you are inculcating is likely to compose 90% of your personality and effectively your position in society, all by the time you are five years old. It is deeply, foundationally ingrained. That's the quite reasonable aim of the parents, and principally it is the quality of the parents - their physical and emotional health, their character and consciousness - that determines the quality of that early personality.

> For instance, in that healthy house, both parents are participating in educating the child that they wanted and planned for. They are playing with him and talking with him, sometimes a little over his head on various topics, to accelerate his understanding of what he needs to know about how life works. How could it be otherwise?
>
> On the other side of town, there's a single mother who didn't want to get pregnant, thought she was safe but wasn't. She lacked the education, training, and interest to properly take care of her child. Worse, but understandably, she feels burdened by him as she is working two jobs just to almost cover basic expenses. She is exhausted and is thankful to have the child plunked down

> in front of television.
>
> The first child is getting timely, quality health care, a nutritious diet, and maybe going to pre-school.
>
> None of that for the other child.
>
> And here's another fact that will determine the children's future. By age four, the uncared for child will have heard 5,000 words spoken to him by his mother and any other people in their life. The other child, with the two parents who have the time and intention to produce a bright child, will by that age have heard 30,000,000 words.

But even in the best of families with the best backgrounds and the best of intentions there is a core problem in the early upbringing of their offspring. They are teaching the child what they believe he needs to learn, based not only on what they were told by their parents but what they have learned during their two or three decades of living their own lives, which probably included learning about taking care of an infant from relatives and friends, training classes and videos. Of course, for the child learning how to communicate, growing his use of letters and numbers to words and sentences and calculations is requisite preparation for school, and for entering the society.

But what about thinking and feeling? When is a child able to learn about these vital internal information processes? What parents know how to explain those essential forms of communication from their own experiences of thinking and feeling without in fact programming their own thoughts and feelings into the child? What parent would even realize how critical it is for a child to be able to experience, define, and value these private, unique, indescribable internal communications?

If this seems oblique, consider that most racism, sexism, ageism, and other brands of discrimination, hatred, fear, and anger get their start in these early years. And it strongly underscores the need to understand how the mind works, and how it is possible to work with thoughts and emotions to make us better people. Also, how to free an individual's mind from outside programming by his parents, friends, community, church, employer, and other social affiliations. Because free, healthy minds are necessary to create a promising future. For them and the world.

And there is this somewhat esoteric point to raise in a discussion of what a child is taught, and that is what does the child already know? It is said that he has access to Jung's *collective unconscious*, an unimaginable wealth of important information. And there are plenty of thoughtful people who suggest that babies are born with the ability to see energy auras around people that reveal their level of consciousness and quality of character.

It is not difficult to suppose that infants come into this world with omniscience, and that it is pushed out of their awareness by all of the immediate lessons they receive from their parents.

> A friend of mine was in a bakery when a young woman came in pushing a carriage with an infant in it. My friend looked at the child, and with a big smile at him said, "Oh you are an old soul, aren't you? Welcome back." The baby responded bright-eyed and gleefully. The mother freaked out and fled with the baby in the carriage.

Dunno. Maybe some of our awareness comes back to us when we are older. And maybe we are seeing it now because we continue to evolve - we never stopped - and to an ever higher level of consciousness.

6 - Energy

> *Seeing is believing, but sometimes the most real things in the world are the things we can't see.*
> *- "The Polar Express"*

Throughout evolution, human consciousness has grown. That growth has been limited, even retarded, by our need to maintain social affiliations. If we did not go along with the isms of our family, our school, our workplace, and especially our church, we were in trouble. In earlier times, we wouldn't have survived. That's still true in more fundamentalist and violent societies today. But since you are reading this book, it's reasonable to presume that you are of a more advanced consciousness.

So, here's a brief talk about physics, or more specifically, the energy that is what and who we are. The *what* is that our body - every physical part of us - is comprised of atoms and atoms are energy. Certainly the *who* of us - our thoughts and our feelings - is energy.

You are likely to remember from not so long ago when people spoke of *body-mind-spirit*. Many people still do. While it was accepted as gospel, and still goes unexamined today, we might consider those words in a reverse order, that is, *spirit-mind-body*.

Why this is significant is that in the old order, we put the *body* in charge, the *mind* cogitating, and the *spirit* cheered or depressed by what the mind reported.

In the updated order, we put the *spirit* speaking to the *mind* which is acting on the *body*. The *spirit* is thoughts and emotions. It is read by the *mind* which has the capacity to initiate changes in the *body*. And it's all energy - our thinking and feeling, the currency of our mind, and the resultant assembly of energy we view as our body.

We know the action and the effects of energy. Even if we can't see the energy itself, we see what it produces when we turn on a light or start a car. Physicists might have a problem with this, but in terms of our perceptions, you might think of it this way ... that energy slows down to become light and then slows down further to become physical matter. Maybe it doesn't slow down except in our perception. What's important to realize is that all of life is energy.

And here is where it gets serious: You have control over how that energy is managed and it starts in the womb. There are various indications that the fetal mind is acquiring information at some point in the mother. For better or ill, depending on the conditions of the trip.

> A vivid example of this energy is a story about a conductor for a major symphony who was holding a rehearsal. He had before him a piece of music he had never seen before. But when he opened it, to his great surprise he found that he knew the score cold. How could that have happened? It turned out that his mother was a concert cellist, and when he was in her womb, she had practiced and played the music many times.

Music is energy, and in quality form, wrote William Congreve three centuries ago, "Music has charms to soothe a savage breast."

7 - The Stage

Give me a place to stand, and I will move the earth. – Archimedes

Most people, in contravention of society's accepted view of reality, believe in ESP, UFOs, and angels, and the vast majority of people around the world believe in some sort of afterlife. Is it out of a need to have a framework of belief; a spiritual element in one's life? Is it self-delusion? Or is it reality?

Are we bound for heaven or hell? Or another life? Or do we just die? For that matter, what are we now?

While some people point to religion, and others prefer The Universe or The Cosmos to explain what is beyond their description. It does seem that there is something bigger than ourselves, and I refer to whatever it is as *the larger reality*. (No capital letters; it's too big to need them.)

There must be a larger reality. Otherwise, what's going on? How else do we describe you and me in the here and now? It isn't plausible that your comprehension of this sentence is the result of some 15 billion years of random combining of amino acids and synapses to produce this moment.

* * * * *

I never believed in a god. Religion seemed like a lifeboat for people who wouldn't take responsibility for their own lives. But I was in my thirties when I began to think that there was something I sensed that I didn't know about but that had significance in my life. This something was affecting my life and likely those of other people, whether they knew it or not, sensed it or not.

As I came to know people of a higher consciousness, that speculation grew. Not because they were selling me anything, just that they were making sense in the issues they parsed and the quality of their thinking. It wasn't until twenty years later that I came up with the term, the larger reality, and it was at that point that I had a vague description of it as a higher dimension that we couldn't see but we could certainly see its touch. Kind of like people saying they saw footprints of Sasquatch, only we really did.

There have been many experiences in my life that have caused me, looking for an explanation of their similar qualities, to arrive at explanations that fit them all and in a simple way ... Coincidence, Purpose, and Consciousness.

These experiences led me to deepen my realization of the larger reality as a creative force that engages those who are *conscious* enough to realize what is happening. That producing *coincidences* that were far larger than the word and beyond any other explanation, must have meaning. And it obviously must have been organized for a *purpose.*

And in answering the question of why were there these experiences, the only explanation was that they were to persuade, and then subsequently affirm, the existence of a creative force.

And as the coincidences and the existence of the purposeful force were personal and positive, it came to me that understanding the *what* it was that was making the coincidences was secondary to the fact that whatever *it* was, was favorable to the participants in the coincidence. It meant to the participants that the coincidence was an affirmation that they were on the right track, and that they should apply themselves to continue to ennoble their character.

Two other points became clear. First was that it's not about believing something. It's something that one is conscious of. The second was that I noticed that coincidences were more frequent, although not necessarily important in their meaningfulness, other than underscoring the path to higher consciousness.

And lately there has come an interesting new perception, maybe dark, maybe hopeful: Considering the rise of insanity and violence, here and around the world, it is probably relevant that there is also a significant surge of higher consciousness.

8 - Of Two Minds ... or More

Inspiration does not come like a bolt, nor is it kinetic, energetic striving, but it comes into us slowly and quietly and all the time, though we must regularly and every day give it a little chance to start flowing, prime it with a little solitude and idleness. – Brenda Ueland

During your early years, when you were getting the lay of the land, you developed a character to deal with the world ... people, situations, unknowns. It was your Ego or personality. It had a preset attitude to meet people you already knew - positive or negative - or strangers of various types new to you. With the negative or unknown, your Ego would likely present a defensive or a protective positive. With familiar and friendly acquaintances, you would display a genial persona.

When you look it up on Google, it says Ego is "a person's sense of self-esteem or self-importance." Ouch. Then it says, in psychoanalytic terms, Ego is "the part of the mind that mediates between the conscious and the unconscious and is responsible for reality testing and a sense of personal identity." Hah! That's a lot closer to what is the role of the Ego. As said earlier, the Ego is what we create as an interface between our self and the rest of the world, and in fond moments we might rather refer to it as our personality.

The Ego's scripts were developed and amended over time as you thought fitting as situations changed. They became so familiar - they were in use during all your waking minutes - that for most people the Ego became the person, to the point that there was little or no variance in the character they presented.

Because the mind is set to default to the Ego, except when you are asleep, can you change that? Not have it be the default? Yes, by going deeper into the earliest conscious mind, for that is where the Ego was built ... by you.

But first, you should understand that there is another character behind the Ego's mask. It is the Ego's creator ... the True Self. Sometimes called the soul, it is the centerpiece of the mind. It is the source of all information coming in and going out. The information coming in is from the senses and from your universe, including what Jung referred to as the *collective unconscious*, which holds all of the information from all time.

Not only is it the source of unlimited information, but it is all true. Not only true but untainted, unless the Ego edits it as it is going out. Whether the information goes out from the True Self clean and true, or it is played with by the Ego is determined in the mind. There can also be half-truths, for instance, when you don't want to hurt someone's feelings.

The True Self is in alignment with the universe. The Ego is not in alignment with the universe because you created it to deal with your outside world.

* * * * *

When you are centered in your True Self, you discover a space between where your mind has the opportunity to intervene. In one instance, I was walking on the boardwalk between the Spanish Bay resort and the beach. It seemed that I would continue on the straight path. But when I got to an intersection with another path that made a ninety degree right turn toward the beach, I took the turn without thinking. I made the decision at a deeper level. I was not only not aware of making the decision to turn, I also had no thought as to why I made the turn. Except that it was a demonstration of the gap between intention and action. I had intended to go straight when I made the turn.

What was particularly noteworthy about the turn was that I experienced no sense of momentum taking me forward. I made the turn without feeling any lateral adjustment. That would defy physics except that in some part of my mind, the decision had been made and weight shift was accounted for.

Another example of this space was when I was sitting at my desk, and I decided to go to the kitchen to get a cup of coffee. I thought that I had given my body the instruction to stand, but in the space between the instruction and the action, I instead canceled the order without being consciously aware of doing so.

There have been more occasions when I have watched myself making decisions that I was not actually conscious of making. An example was when I was looking at some shirts hanging in the closet. I reached out for the shirt I thought I had decided to wear, but I watched as I reached for a different shirt. I was not conscious of either making a decision or changing it.

More than once I was going to take something from the refrigerator and instead I walked out of the kitchen, again without a thought about it in my conscious mind.

It's not that these were important decisions. It is important that I was not conscious of making them. That a different part of my mind was involved. I surmise that this non-cognitive part of my mind that acted is directly connected to the larger reality. It may be an aspect of what we refer to as a sixth sense. There is more on a sixth sense in Chapter 23.

9 - The New World

I am irritated by my own writing. I am like a violinist whose ear is true, but whose fingers refuse to reproduce precisely the sound he hears within. - Gustave Flaubert

I was brought up in New England by a semi-Freudian psychoanalyst father and a mother who was a writer called the Jane Austin of the twentieth century in her obituary written by her esteemed publisher who adored her. A very intellectual family - I was sent to Exeter - and not only was there no religion but also no spirituality. You live, you die, you molder in the grave, and you work hard in between.

I was following that track. I was a producer for ABC Network Television News, earning a handful of national awards, vacationing in the Caribbean, and nicely set in a co-op apartment a block from Central Park. But I was serious about journalism, and in the late 70s, Roone Arledge, who had made a success of the network's sports coverage was given control of the news department as well. He was more interested in the sizzle than the steak.

So in the fall of 1980, I quit and moved from the concrete canyons of Manhattan to the redwood canyons of Mill Valley, just over the Golden Gate Bridge from San Francisco in marvy Marin County. It was more than changing coasts. I dove into a very different world.

Not just the peacock feathers and hot tubs. It was about a truly new way of thinking which I learned much about while reading *The Tao of Psychology*, *The Aquarian Conspiracy*, *Chop Wood Carry Water,* and several short but remarkably informative books on human psychology from the Jungian therapist Robert A. Johnson. All the books were very important. They were not selling adherence, just higher consciousness. I have reread most of them, and some a number of times, and recently.

Anyway, in a short time I was out of my new job as a newswriter for a local television station, a new marriage was over after four months, and I was running out of money. No wonder I looked around for some answers, and I looked to people whose ideas had been light targets of humor in my previous life.

I had a session each with an astrologer, a psychic, and a palm reader. None of them knew me before the short time - maybe a half-hour - that I spent with them. They knew virtually nothing about me, only my name and date of birth. (The three people who recommended them to me knew very little about me.)

So how could I explain that each of them told me the same three specific aspects about me the first and only time I ever met them? Dunno, but they did. First was that I had a difficult relationship with my father. Second was that I had to live near water. And the third was that I would help to change the world through communications.

Well, one and two were surely spot on, and as for the third, back forty years ago, the Earth was indeed very different with three billion fewer people on it. Life made more sense back then, or at least it seemed manageable. But in regard my helping making to change the world through communications ... I'm still working on it.

More to the point, my thinking needed some serious updating. Life no longer made sense the way I had been approaching it. My curiosity about this new world of very different thinking led me to meet some interesting people who, recognizing my hunger to find a new way, gave me conversation, recommended important reading, and patiently engaged my impatient questions. Impatient because I had so much ground to turn over and dig into, and there were no magic pills.

10 - Magic People

If you're always trying to be normal you will never know how amazing you can be.
- Maya Angelou

They weren't magic, but from a number of people I met in my first few years of living in Marin County I learned a lot that changed my life. One was a psychologist who I knew as a friend, not a patient. His name was John, but his last name escapes me some 40 years later.

John introduced me to the first two books by Robert A. Johnson, *She: Understanding Feminine Psychology* and *He: Understanding Masculine Psychology*. I read them back then and have reread them over the years since. They are short, clear, and rich in valuable perspective information, as were the other ten of his books that I also read.

- Robert A. Johnson was a noted Jungian analyst and lecturer, and his books have sold over 2.5 million copies. Those books are both brilliant and fairly easy to understand in his explanation of important aspects of human psychology. He also drops wonderful tidbits into his treatises that will stay with you forever. For instance, in *Transformation: Understanding the Three Levels of Masculine Consciousness,* in which he uses Don Quixote, Hamlet, and Faust in illuminating the three levels of male consciousness, Johnson wrote, "I inquired into the origin of the word *happy* and found that it derives from the verb to happen. In other words, happiness is to be found simply from observing what happens. If you cannot be happy at the prospect of lunch, you are not likely to find happiness anywhere. What happens is happiness."

In *He: Understanding Masculine Psychology,* which I found ever more important each time I read it, Johnson looked at the word enthusiasm, which he broke down in Greek as *en-theo-ism* which means to be filled with God. Of course a person can be filled with various sorts of transient or lifelong goals or purposes. Artists can be flooded with the need to create, athletes compelled to make a better score, a teacher to engage his students in gaining knowledge, a doctor to heal his patients. The nine Muses are pushing them/us to greater accomplishment.

In several of his books, Johnson speaks of the ability to live with paradox ... to realize that contending truths can coexist. "Heroism could be redefined for our time as the ability to stand paradox." He offers the example of living in the light and knowing we have a stake in darkness. "Until we have undertaken the task of accepting and honoring the shadow within us, we cannot be balanced or whole, for what is hidden never goes away, but - often painfully - turns up in unexpected places."

He notes, bluntly, "When the unstoppable bullet hits the impenetrable wall, we find the religious experience." And he sees such trying times as an opening for true growth, an "invitation to that, which is greater than oneself."

- David Spangler was another important contact. Not knowing anything about him, I was somehow induced to attend a Sunday afternoon lecture he gave at the Tiburon Community Church. I'd not heard of Spangler and had never been to the church; I wasn't to go there again. I note that for the uniqueness of the occasion.

Spangler had helped to establish Findhorn as a residential center for spiritual education. Considered one of the early founders of the modern New Age, he later became critical of some in the movement who were becoming too commercial and sensational.

Anyway, that Sunday afternoon Spangler talked about our growth in consciousness. From what I remember, the first of five stages is when an infant realizes the existence of his self. In the second stage, he realizes that his world divides into himself and Other; i.e., everything and everyone else. In the third stage, he begins to create his personality to deal with Other. As he winds up living in his personality for most of his waking hours, the personality is pretty much his life.

From his experience and the inherent expansion of the personality's control, most people spend little conscious time on their original Self. For most people, this is their fourth stage.

But some are on another path. They are open to the concept of the Self. That being open means more experiences of higher intelligence, a stronger sense of character, and a growing realization of the potential of the Self. And the more one engages that deeper part of his Self, the more he finds it very much to his benefit. The building of the Self is the fourth stage.

In the fifth stage comes the recognition of the spiritual connection between Self and Other.

Then and today, Spangler's explanation struck me as a vital map of understanding our growth in terms of consciousness.

- José Argüelles was another important figure in the New Age. He was the author of *The Mayan Factor: Path Beyond Technology*. We met several times and at one point he induced me fly to Dallas to speak at a peace conference hosted by Robert Muller, the author of *Most of All, They Taught Me Happiness.*

– And there was Charles Garfield, best known for his work on peak performance, he himself was a peak performer of international note. A former world-class weightlifter, he started his professional life as a mathematician, working on the NASA team that sent Apollo 11 to the moon. Then he got a PhD in psychology which he applied to the patients and medical personnel who were dealing with cancer. His efforts helped to establish the Shanti Projects.

I became friends with Charlie and Cindy Spring, his prime associate who later became his wife. I wound up producing a video profile of Charlie's extraordinary experience and skill set that he would use to open top corporate doors.

* * * * *

These people were valuable mentors for me, in books and in person. We don't seem to appreciate the importance of mentoring, maybe because it doesn't have much accessible form. Perhaps the lack of form is a clue of where we are today.

A healthy attitude is to keep your eyes open for a possible mentor. Mentors can be sitting at the next desk; they can come from very different lives. They can offer instruction for years, or just for a short time, but what they have to say to you can move you in a direction or enhance your thinking about a subject important to your future. Or maybe polish up your presentation skills.

If you find someone you sense has information for you - static or training - you might see if there is a fit. This note: rarely should a relationship be forced. For the most part, mentors are natural givers.

* * * * *

Writing about mentors reminded me of George Mellor. He was the director of the Lamont Art Gallery at Exeter, and he became a close friend and mentor. On one occasion he recommended that I leave Exeter for a weekend. This was allowed by the school, but I had to have previously made travel arrangements. I hadn't. George said, "Go ahead, do something wrong. "

And I did. I thumbed home - a major no-no - on a weekend my parents were in New York. I took their other car and drove a hundred miles each way to see a girlfriend at her boarding school for an hour or so and drove home.

My parents came home the next day and my father was furious. And maybe for the first time, I didn't let his anger bother me. In fact, and this is going back more than 50 years, my attitude induced him to actually be gracious as he drove me to the bus to get back to school.

11 - On the Mat

Let the rain kiss you.
Let the rain beat upon your head
with silver liquid drops.
Let the rain sing you a lullaby.
- Langston Hughes

Perhaps the most valued mentors I met were on the mat. The mat is where I learned and trained in *aikido*.

> Aikido is a 20th century martial art. Aikido is three words ai-ki-do which mean "the harmonious blending of energy as a way of being." An aikidoist uses an attacker's energy to disarm the attack. The aim is to find a peaceful resolution ... if possible.

And it was on the mat at the Aikido of Tamalpais *dojo* (training center) that I met some people who were instrumental in my spiritual grounding and moving me toward a new understanding of who I was, and what choices I had.

One in particular was George Leonard, a wartime Air Force fighter pilot, the editor of *Look* magazine, and President Emeritus of the Esalen Institute. He was also a fifth-degree aikido black belt and founder of the Aikido of Tamalpais dojo. He developed the Leonard Energy Training (LET), non-falling practice for centering the mind, body, and spirit, and was a prolific author of important books including *Education and Ecstasy, The Transformation,* and *The Silent Pulse.*

I learned a lot from George. He had me read one of his manuscripts before it was ready for the printer. He was not only a generous teacher, but he was a dear friend. I enjoyed a number of Thanksgivings and Christmases at his home.

* * * * *

An important gift he gave his LET students was to understand *soft eyes*. What he meant by soft eyes was to let your eyes go out of hard focus so they can take in more. It's the difference between looking and seeing. Understand that what you are looking at is .003% of what your eyes are seeing. Your mind reports to you everything your eyes are seeing, but in most situations, you will be better off using soft eyes to see more.

You can expand the soft concept to your ears. With *soft ears* you can pick up more sounds. Try it out in nature and you will be amazed at what you will hear, from the wind airing out the flora, to sounds of the fauna, including small animals on the ground in the bushes, and the birds in the trees and flying by in the air.

And then there is *soft mind*. An open mind. One without the hard-edged limitations created by a particular focus. Also in this state, you can clear your mind of unproductive or useless thoughts. With the soft mind you can expand the scope of what you are contemplating. It gives you a richer palette of ideas that can add depth to your perception. And not only does soft mind broaden your reach, it can also bring you what you need to see into sharper focus.

It is also effortless. In soft mind, you can access your universe, all knowledge, Jung's *collective unconscious*. Not only access, but in soft mind, you can identify key points in the subject for your study.

Soft mind can be particularly valuable when you are confused or undecided. Going into soft mind enables you to let go of presumptions, which are most likely blocking your path. Most decisions are based on a number of suppositions, some that you never questioned. Some that deserve questioning and mitigation.

* * * * *

George was famous for repeating the dictum when training in aikido, to attack your opponent in a serious way; don't lighten up on the strikes. Because it does little good to learn how to deal with a less than strong attack. Which is why he would advise the recipient to "Take the hit as a gift."

This applies equally off the aikido mat and in life. When you feel that you are suffering a "hit" - e.g., facing against a wall - take it as a gift. Instead of trying to move forward, you might take a step backward. And while you will still see the wall in front of you, you will see a window on one side and a door on the other.

* * * * *

One of the most valuable energy tools I learned from George was how to prevent anger and other negative energy from having a weighty effect on me. He stood twelve feet away from me and told me to stand strong and firm. When I was ready, he charged toward me, stopping only inches away. I felt the energy of his "attack" very strongly. It took some effort to keep my place.

Then George repositioned himself and instructed me to change my posture from strong and firm to feeling wide open, like a screen door. Then he charged toward me forcefully again. This time, I let his energy go through me and felt no challenge to keeping my balance.

You can do that when you are feeling verbally assaulted, just by being the screen door and letting the energy - anger or even just annoyance or rudeness

– pass through you without effect. The importance of this is that when the attack is over and has had no effect, the attacker's energy is gone or at least defused. That creates space for mediation or walking away.

*   *   *   *   *

In one of George's books, I think it was *The Silent Pulse: A Search for the Perfect Rhythm that Exists in Each of Us*, he reported on a most interesting lab test. Using a fast-action camera, they shot two men having a conversation. When they examined the film they found that during the conversation, the speaker at one point used the word "ask". Because it was several times faster than normal film, they found that the word broke down into five separate sounds. What they discovered was that the speaker made a different set of physical moves in conjunction with each of those five sounds. What was even more amazing was that the listener also made five different sets of physical moves with the five different sounds, in direct synchrony with the speaker's sound and moves. That discovery speaks volumes about the human mind and energy.

*   *   *   *   *

There was another lesson that George used to show how some people's minds work. He had some 16 people in his energy class. He told them to stay where they were standing on the mat, and with their eyes closed, to turn slowly in place. Then he added that if they felt a soft tap on their shoulder, they were to stop turning, open their eyes, look straight ahead for just a fraction of a second, and quickly close their eyes. Then they should continue turning slowly in place.

The turning in place went on for several minutes and then George had everyone stop turning, open their eyes, and sit on the mat. He talked for a few moments about how the mind works, and then he asked if anyone had experienced something strange during the exercise. None of the students, all adults of various ages, said they had. George then asked the people who had felt a tap on their shoulder to raise their hand; four of them did, tentatively. He asked them if they hadn't seen a strange mask when they opened their eyes. They agreed that they had. George had stood before each of the four with a funny mask on his face. He explained that it's often difficult for people to register something that doesn't fit into what they know.

* * * * *

Robertson Davies, a wonderful writer and a great thinker, noted in his first novel, *Tempest-Tost,* "The eye sees only what the mind is prepared to comprehend." That's particularly important, especially when the mind is closed. A person can't entertain new ideas that challenge what he thinks he knows and lives by, e.g., religion, corporate rules, social dictum. They are unwilling to hear the truth.

Another example of the truth of Davies comment is in this from *Silent Alarm*, a novel I wrote in 1985:

> "When you go to sleep, your cognitive lobe ceases to dominate. It's present and active, of course, but it doesn't dominate. What happens is you oscillate between your right and left, your intuitive and cognitive, so quickly that it is virtually simultaneous. Your right side lets in the energy from the universe, and the left converts the energy into images or ideas that the mind can grasp."
>
> "Is that why sometimes I dream of people or situations that don't exist in real life?"
>
> "That's right. Your left lobe does its best to translate the energy into a recognizable context, but sometimes it can't. When you're awake, the cognitive lobe insists on forcing the energy into some acceptable definition. But when you're sleeping, the left lobe can't dominate, so you get some strange pictures and ideas. That's why it's hard for a lot of people to remember their dreams: the images don't fit into their *awake reality*."
>
> "The not remembering is a form of denial then?"
>
> "Yes, in a way."

12 - Wendy Palmer

This is a new year. A new beginning. And things will change. – Taylor Swift

Another important figure in my life in Mill Valley was Wendy Palmer, a co-founder with George Leonard of the Aikido of Tamalpais dojo. She was a very fine aikido *sensei* or instructor, and a wonderful personal instructor for me, not only in aikido but also in understanding energy. One cold morning we were alone in the dojo, sitting on the mat in a spot which the sun was hitting through a window.

She had me close my eyes, relax, breathe deeply and slowly, and clear my mind. After a few quiet moments, she asked me if I saw anything. I told her that I saw a single black rose on a blue background. Wendy was very quiet. Then she told me that she had been thinking of a good friend who had cancer.

After a few moments, we rose and she had us walk together around the mat, she holding my elbow gently, and I walking with my eyes closed. I recounted to her what I was seeing. I can see it all today, 40 years later.

> I am moving along a beam of yellow golden light. It leads ahead of me like a pathway, but when I look down, it's just a large cylindrical beam of light. And I'm not walking, because I don't have a body. I feel ethereal. My presence is very strong, but I don't seem to have any physical form.
>
> There is no ground or floor below, no sky above. The beam is in the middle of a beautiful bright white-yellow light realm; bright but not glaring and soft in a way that I don't have to squint. I can see stars or sparkles of some sort, golden and white, twinkling all about. And there are rainbows flowing through in the distant background.
>
> I am "walking" along this beam toward something small and dark. It grows larger as I near it, and I can see that it looks like the opening of a tunnel. As I get closer, I can see that it is a portal into a realm of darkness. There are very few stars in that darkness; it is like nighttime.
>
> Now I have a body. I am standing in the portal, my feet lightly braced on the bottom of the circle; my arms are stretched out to a relaxed distance as my hands hold onto the top of the circle. I'm half in the light and half in the darkness. Wendy asks if I am going to enter the darkness. I tell her

> I don't know how. She asks, "What happens if I you just let go?"
>
> Which I do, and I fall, not down but weightlessly into the darkness; I'm in something of a loose, fetal crouch. There is no feeling of danger or being lost, just quiet.

At that point, we stopped walking around the mat. I opened my eyes. Wendy didn't ask me what I thought of the experience, and I wouldn't have had anything else to tell her at that point. It would take some time to process. But I did later. I thought it must be a metaphor of my birth.

Many years later ...

> I was sitting on a bench by the ocean in Pebble Beach when I remembered that experience with Wendy. I closed my eyes and cleared my mind. After a short while, I had an image looking out at the scene that was actually the one in front of me. But then my view changed. It got small as it seemed as if I had been looking through a hole in a fence, maybe a knothole in a plank in the fence, except that I pulled back from the view through the hole, and it got smaller and smaller until it closed. I suddenly realized that I was in full darkness, again with a very few stars, like what I had entered when I left the bright white-yellow light realm when I was walking with Wendy.

Maybe that was my death. It looked like the right

way to go, very peaceful, though I was aware in that moment that I wasn't in a hurry to experience it.

* * * * *

One more story about the Aikido of Tamalpais dojo back around 1983.

> It was a bad day. Late one morning I returned from a meeting in the city where my attorney had persuaded me that I had no choice but to pay off my divorcing wife of just a few months with an outrageous sum of money.
>
> The night before, I learned that my youngest sister had gotten a bad pap smear.
>
> And early that morning, I read that a woman friend, only 30 years old, had shot herself to death in a motel room.
>
> Instead of going home, I headed to the dojo. I had no specific purpose in mind. Nor did I have any reason to think that it would even be open. However, there was a note saying, "Tony, the door is open." It was. I went in and punched away on a punching bag for twenty minutes, not something I had ever done before. And exhausted but with a feeling of release, I was done. I never found out who had left the note.

* * * * *

And there's this story of what being on-the-mat did

for me. My usual training schedule was five to six in the afternoon. So when I saw that it was five minutes until the end of class, I started to relax out of my aikido state of mind. But then Wendy called a final exercise. And with my mind somewhere between training and being finished with aikido for the day, I stood quietly present as my *uke*, my training partner, attacked me. Without tensing, without thinking, I deflected the attack and pinned him on the mat. It was such a "thoughtless" act I was startled.

It opened a view of my mind that I wanted to be able to get to deliberately and on my cue. I have subsequently gone to that place, not in a physical confrontation, and not deliberately, but in conversation. It is happening with ever greater frequency. I believe it is switching out of the Ego mind of deliberate thought to the free spirit voice of the True Self.

(There is more about who Wendy Palmer is, the important books she has written, and the groundbreaking work that she is doing in the Appendix.)

13 - What Time Is It?

Except for the point,
the still point,
there would be no dance,
and there is only the dance.
- T.S. Eliot

It was February 1982, and I was on my first trip back to Northampton, Massachusetts to visit my family since I'd moved to the West Coast. It was for my sister Maggie's wedding. It was a grand weekend, and everyone had gone their own way by Monday. I was to leave the next day. My mother and I spent much of the day together, and that evening we were sitting together in the kitchen talking. I reprised to her how my father had been unhappy with me the night of my arrival when I mentioned Carl Jung's name. I had recently learned - sketchily - some of Jung's ideas, but I hadn't known that my psychoanalyst father was not one of his fans.

To say the least. Which is sort of how he showed it, when with a frown he said, "I hope you're not going to bring him up with me."

Surprised, I winced and shook my head, smiled and gracefully turned away to talk to another of my family. Not about Jung.

Anyway, back to that Monday and I guess I was expressing my disappointment with my father when all I was doing was talking about what a new world I was finding in Mill Valley. My mother seemed resistant, and I made the mistake of pursuing the track. I asked her if she loved me.

She said, "Of course."

"As your son?"

"Yes."

"As a person?"

"I don't know you as a person."

"Do you want to know who I am?"

She didn't know.

I was irked. I had been exposed to some very interesting new ideas that I wanted to share, and I felt shut out. And mostly because my mother was a serious intellectual. An author of a number of books, one of which was a finalist for the 1977 National Book Award for Fiction. She should be open to hearing about some of the discoveries her son was making. I don't know if she just wasn't interested or if she was concerned that I would challenge what she thought she knew. Anyway, the conversation became impatient and then moved to angry.

Finally, to her surprise and mine, she ordered me to leave the house. I went upstairs and started packing my things. She followed me up shortly and told me she didn't want me to leave that way. I apologized, we hugged, and everything was forgiven. But not forgotten.

It was the following October when I got a call from one of my sisters that my mother, after having Hodgkin's Disease for almost twelve years was coming to the end of her life. I flew east the next day. My mother was in a coma. I went to the hospital to see her every day, but nothing had changed. Then on the Monday night before the Saturday morning when she passed, I sat on the edge of her bed and leaned over to kiss her goodnight on her forehead.

Suddenly she opened her eyes and looked up at me, as healthy as could be, with a warm smile. I was startled and delighted.

"What time is it?" she asked me.

I turned my head to see the clock on the opposite wall, turned back to her and reported, "It's ten-oh-six."

Her smile widened slightly, and she said, looking into my eyes, "You're right." Then she closed her eyes, never to open them again.

I knew in that moment that she was referring to our talk the previous February. It took me a while to understand that she had been to the other side and seen enough to realize that what I had tried to talk to her about, clumsy as I had been having just scratched the surface of what I was learning and wanted to explain, had validity. As my awareness grew, the importance of that experience grew within me. Her coming back after being in a coma for five days was a great gift for both of us.

14 - The Incredible Mind

It's better to create something that others criticize than to create nothing and criticize others. – Ricky Gervais

Some people with lazy, little-used minds, say that human beings are essentially limited to see, hear, taste, smell, and touch, and for them it is close to the truth. So where do ideas come from? The mind, of course. It is fed by our five senses but there is a constant flow of information that runs from our True Self, our principle source of thoughts in the form of intuition, and feelings that arrive through instinct. Our mind works with all the "raw materials" and a limitless library of information from our experiences and knowledge, along with the collective unconscious. The mind imagines, manipulates, and otherwise processes the information to produce what we know as our consciousness. It's an ongoing process every moment of our existence.

The more you know yourself, the more information you will receive about what you are capable of.

You've probably heard people say that "You only use 8% of your brain." That's just a popular toss-off. Most of the brain is used, but much of the time it seems that most people aren't using any of theirs.

But this is where the confusion about the brain and the mind gets cleared up because while they may be using most or all of their brain, their mind is AWOL. In truth, too often it seems that the vast majority of our species doesn't begin to use their mind anywhere near their potential. As explained earlier, it's because the incredible expanse of knowledge with which we come into this world has been pushed out of our close awareness with the inculcation of well-meaning but typically inaccurate and/or outdated information from our parents, siblings, and others in our first few years.

But as people experience and reacquire some of the vast amount of far more valuable information available in higher consciousness, the mind is re-awakened and in many different ways, both in dealing with the outside world, and especially with the inner workings of the mind.

I've talked about interpreting dreams and feelings; with higher consciousness you may also find that you are able to be aware of your dreams as you are dreaming them. It is like you are of two minds, but in fact, it's your one amazing mind displaying its incredible facility of operating on multiple tracks simultaneously.

Of course we are using multiple tracks all the time. When we're driving, we don't consciously calculate how much to turn the steering wheel and how much to press down on the accelerator or switch to the brake. That's handled without cognitive thought. That's different from the brain, which is running our organs, breathing, swallowing, blinking, et cetera. Those are basically autotomic actions, while the mind focuses on staying within your lane at 65 mph, appreciating the music playing on the flash drive, and engaging in conversation with your passenger.

* * * * *

Yes, we take all that for granted, but it is just a part of what the mind is truly capable of, and to your benefit. And as you open your mind to the possibilities - that you can't begin to imagine - you will get more guidance. You have to pay attention.

Here's a simple example. When I was about to drive a half-hour away to get my second COVID vaccination, the thought occurred to me that I should bring a book with me in case there was a wait. Actually, the thought came to me twice. But both times I argued down the "suggestion" citing my experience the first time I'd driven up for a shot and there had been no time to fill. I decided I wouldn't need a book. But this time there was more than an hour of waiting in line in my car, due to some organizing snafu.

I should have listened. But the fact that I didn't, made me aware that I shouldn't have to hear such a suggestion a second time when it comes to me the way that it did. Who was I, what did I think I knew, to ignore that "voice" again?

Since then, I've recognized the messaging a good number of times and have always responded. It not only served my purposes, it reenforced the value of listening to it. And with it each time came a sense of deeper respect, and a softer peace. One particularly relevant example is that when I was starting to put this book together, I heard the voice tell me to re-read *Mokki's Peak.* Actually, I had to hear it more than once. Then I read it. As you will see later in this book, it was a good thing I finally listened.

* * * * *

Where do ideas come from? Two sources: the True Self (or soul) which sources your unique individual universe, and the Ego, which is your own work, created to interface with the outside world; both are resident in the mind. What comes from the True Self is true and productive. What comes from the Ego might need examination to confirm that it has such qualities in the moment. Depending on what level of consciousness you have reached, it could well be that you are seriously self-aware and your Ego contributes useful ideas, based on the truth and clear experiences of outside input.

Ideas might also be a complex of more than one input. Ideas can be new, especially in fresh or unfamiliar circumstances. They can also be recovered from a long time ago or reassembled from various bits of information that you acquired previously from other sources, with or without an add-on by you.

* * * * *

What is an open mind? Openness is relative. You are not going to be open to what you consider absurd or to be false. But having an open mind means that you are more willing to consider information you have previously rejected either because you have gained new information and/or it is coming from a source in which you have faith or trust.

When considering new or resurfaced ideas to embrace or discard, it is not something to rush through. Remember, you are usually dealing with new material with a somewhat split view, your Ego and your True Self. Your Ego is going to be very protective of what you think you know. After all, who wants to be shown to have been wrong.

Your True Self will report the facts, but there is still no need to make a hurried evaluation of it. First, because you can gain from the internal dialogue over the two views and learn from less obvious details. The second reason for taking your time is that whatever the issue, whether or not it is new to you, you are likely to be seeing it with an overlay of your intrinsic presumptions. What may not look like the right track to follow on a particular issue might look better through new glasses. Similarly, what might not seem a wrong track could be clouded by a preset opinion. With a freshly opened mind, what does your instinct tell you?

*   *   *   *   *

What determines what ideas come to our mind that are deserving of our attention? Having an open mind enables a broader range of thoughts coming to our attention. Having one or more particular subjects or questions will also invite related thoughts to come to mind. Sort of like how a thesaurus will present a variety of alternatives that can be close or totally wrong from what you were seeking. But we also might get a great idea because we are looking for an unrelated solution.

An idea might pop into our head (figuratively) because it speaks to an ongoing area of interest. It will not infrequently be that a thought will arise that is not important but appears because of a misunderstanding or confusion on our part on a related matter. The more we keep a healthy, open mind the more often thoughts that further our purpose will come to mind.

*   *   *   *   *

While the mind has its own authority, we can exercise it in difference ways. Consider that you are reading a book and while your eyes remain on the page, your mind goes off thinking about something else, often on an entirely different track from what you were reading. When you come back from the something else, you find yourself seeing the text again and realizing that you haven't read it and have to find the place where you left off in thought. It dramatically reveals the mind's priority over what the eyes were focused on.

I remember experiencing thoughts coming through to my attention like a series of slides going through a viewer rapidly one at a time without stopping. It happened because I deliberately gave none of them my attention. I think we may be doing that often but not being aware of it because we are in fact sorting through them and passing on those that don't need or deserve our attention, at least at the moment. This suggests that our mind is choosing what we should be thinking about. That makes sense.

I think it was Deepak Chopra who said that we maybe have 60,000 thoughts a day. The slide show I experienced is a metaphor for our ability to select or ignore thoughts as they present themselves. It underscores the fact that the thoughts we choose to receive our attention describe our consciousness. In effect, they define us.

The more conscious person is going to clear his mind of thoughts that are of little or no value to make room for new thoughts that are worthy of their attention. Part of the parsing is to not waste time on matters that will only be distractions from what you have been working on.

That said, a distraction might have its own purpose, at least for a short time. I often find it useful to my thought process, like writing this book, to take a break. Maybe get a cup of coffee or go for a long walk. Returning to the writing, I inevitably have a refreshed mind.

15 - Thoughts and Feelings

I have had my results for a long time: but I do not yet know how I am to arrive at them.
- Carl Friedrich Gauss

Here's some new math for you, only it doesn't involve numbers. Rather, the factors are thoughts, feelings, and knowledge:

To Think +To Feel = To Know

Typically, the animus, or primary male energy, has been funneled into thinking, calculating, and planning. Just as the anima, or female energy, has predominantly gone into feeling, emotions, and facilitation. Both genders have some of the other's energy too. That's why most people have a natural mixture of predilections and skills. It is a mixture of those energies - in an individual or a couple or a group - that makes it more likely to produce a more holistic, richer knowledge of a situation. It is why a healthy relationship is often with individuals understanding their differences and balancing their strengths of anima and animus so they can cooperate rather than conflict.

> The better you know yourself, the more likely you are to find your mate. If you are portraying yourself through your Ego, you are inviting candidates who are likely to be attracted to how you portray yourself rather than to your True Self.

* * * * *

I went online and typed in the address bar, "What is the opposite of intellect" and in a millisecond or maybe faster, I had the answer: "intellect - opposite - emotion". That was exactly the word I was expecting. I was validated in my view of the vital duality of thoughts and feelings.

We interpret our feelings using thoughts, of course. But feelings are like dreams. We can't make a direct translation from feelings or dreams to thoughts because they are different languages. This can create a serious challenge in our internal dialogue, particularly with feelings. From the beginning of our cognitive experience of feelings – that is, when we understood that we were having feelings and made an effort to identify their meaning – we have labeled feelings in various ways based on our level of consciousness and intellect at the time. (There is more on this subject in Chapter 25 - *The Evolution of the Mind.*)

And therein lies the rub, because we started defining

and labeling very early on, and we have tended to hold onto those shorthand labels to identify those feelings. Most people experienced their primary feelings and defined them before they were five years old. And many people have kept those labels into adulthood and throughout their lives.

This raises two issues. First is that our descriptions of what the feelings mean are very likely out of date, at least, and in the worst case, they could be very wrong. For instance, we can feel happy when we are being spoiled with too much food, and that can lead to obesity. We can very easily have misunderstood various situations and people that we encountered early in life, and labeled the feelings about them inappropriately, either positively or negatively, and we can be misapplying those labels today. And second, we are very likely to skip quickly from the shorthand identification of a feeling and in the process shortchange ourselves of the full examination of what we are feeling.

Why this is so important is that our feelings come from our deepest, most prescient True Self, and to cut them off midway can deprive us of vital information. Feelings come from the same source but in a different format from thoughts. While thoughts come through intuition in words, feelings come through emotionally, instead of verbally, and via instinct. The purpose of two formats is that we are better able to understand messaging in two different ways; stereo instead of mono, if you will.

> A friend was feeling down - she said sad - because she wasn't enjoying a work situation the way she had when she started her job a couple of years earlier. It wasn't about money. Some of the people had left and she didn't have the same feelings about those who had replaced them. They were in no way bad people, they were different, and my friend wasn't enjoying being at the office as she had.
>
> I suggested to her that she might look at her feelings in a different light, that it wasn't sadness but an indication to her that it was simply time to leave. Because in fact, the job required a lot of climbing up and down stairs, and that was producing some physical strain.
>
> She heard what I was saying, but I could see that it was a challenge for her to re-identify the feelings from the negative to a positive.

Our feelings can be reacting to a thought or from reading energy from people and outside circumstances. We can sometimes misread our feelings the way our dreams are often misread. It's less an issue of a different language since our feelings are generated internally.

Misreading can also be due to our predilection toward a person, positive or negative. Our attitude toward a person can set us up for or against what we expect to hear from them. How we read them is very often based on our current frame of mind. Other predilections, particularly of people we don't know well or who are brand new to us, can be formed by age, race, gender, hierarchy, attitude, expectations, life that day, and, of course, our level of consciousness.

* * * * *

What is the purpose of the part of the mind that tees up negative thoughts? Where is that function in us? What feeds it? What stops it? We would like to think that most children are born with a spirit of goodness. That there is a light on inside all of us to begin with. But all too frequently, that light burns out, maybe down to a flicker, from pain and fear, or misunderstanding. We program our mind with expectations based on our experience, starting in the womb and then from our early years to today. The programming is based on our expectation of what we will be dealing with.

> There is a story about the philosopher Abraham Maslow speaking to a class of high school-age British students. He asked, "Who among you is going to be great?" and no one raised their hand. Then he said, "Who else then?"
>
> Now imagine if 18 years earlier, a question was posed to the parents of these children, asking them, "Who of your children is going to be

great?" Wouldn't every hand have gone up? And what then happened in the ensuing 18 years?

Much of the programming that we receive through the years is to protect us. If our circumstances change, so can our expectations. We change those expectations by recognizing our inclinations and then altering our programmed responses.

A common pattern that we have to deal with is one that my mother occasionally accused me of. She said that I heard not what she said but what I wanted to hear. That was either a practice of persuading myself to interpret something she said differently from what she meant, or outright lying on my part. I suppose many children go through a phase of such behavior, and there are certainly enough adults who have a record of hearing "yes" when they were in fact told "no", but that is no surprise. Not to the "no"-sayers.

*   *   *   *   *

We use thoughts to explain our feelings, and we experience feelings to understand our thoughts. What do we think about a feeling? What do we feel about a thought? That can present significant difficulties for a person with a limited vocabulary or consciousness.

The more conscious we are, the better we are at interpreting words and behavior that can produce complex feelings. The more open we are, the better listeners we are, the less confusion there will be.

On the other hand, people who are less self-aware and easily upended, generally tend to default to the negative when receiving unexpected or unclear inputs. Their feelings may be skewed because they don't anticipate change, and if they are disinclined or fear change, they automatically label those feelings as negative.

A healthy frame of mind does not think that everything *will be* all right. It's that everything *is* all right, and we just have to adjust our perspective. It's good to remember, too, that what catches our attention might not be what we're looking for, but it might well be something that is more important.

> The other day the city of Pacific Grove was getting ready to have a pet parade, which meant closing off the main street. Traffic was a mess for four blocks in every direction. I was driving slowly toward my destination when suddenly a person in a parked car started to open his door to the street. I swerved and he closed his door at the same time. Whew! That was close. I just missed hitting his car.

Later I reframed my thought about the near-hit. It wasn't that it was almost a smashed car door. Instead, it *wasn't* a smashed car door. So no "whew," but a smile. I could look at it as having been saved by being on the right track.

Setting out a new way of thinking, one that defaults to a positive perspective, a friend said, "I gotta go there. I gotta be there. I gotta live there." His partner smiled and described it this way: "Everything is good. How do you know it? Where do you know it? I know it more deeply than thinking it." Yup, it's in the True Self where feelings are born.

* * * * *

Almost all minds that can be changed must be reached through emotional channels first, and only then followed with reason. A clear proof was provided by Drew Westen, a professor in the Department of Psychology and Psychiatry at Emory University; he is also a consultant to non-profits and progressive political organizations. I interviewed him in 2007, shortly after he published *The Political Brain*. I asked him about his estimate that 95% of American voters vote their emotions. He hesitated, then replied, "Maybe 96%." But of course! No one votes for someone they don't like, unless they like the opponent even less.

* * * * *

Minds must be changed one at a time through emotional connections first, then followed with thinking. In order to change someone's mind you have to engage him.

It was December 1968, the end of a calamitous year with the assassinations of Martin Luther

King, Jr., and Robert Kennedy, and the election of Richard Nixon as president. I drove from New York, where I was in my freshman year at NYU to Lake Worth, Florida to spend the Christmas holiday with my grandmother. My grandfather had died three years earlier.

Some of the time in Lake Worth I spent driving my grandmother around town, in part so that she could introduce me to people who had known my grandfather. He had made many friends in the 15 years he had lived there. These people not only liked him but respected him. As I always had.

One day my grandmother had me pull into a gas station, and an older fellow came over to my window. He looked probably twenty years older than his actual age, and he didn't have many teeth.

"This is Karl's grandson," my grandmother told him.

The man's expression changed from casual to serious. He looked at me and he said, "Your granddaddy was a great man." He nodded for emphasis, and then told me why. "He taught me to say Nee-gro," he said, underlining the pronunciation, "instead of niggah."

A lot has changed in the last half-century, but too slowly and not enough. Perhaps because such a

> transformation cannot be legislated or simply funded. What is required is a cultural shift instigated by education of one person at a time. Then a family or some friends. But the hatred, the anger, the fear must be mitigated in the heart before the mind will learn.

This from a novel - yes, a novel - on education reform that I wrote in 2018. *The Bright Wise Solution* explains how to open minds through engagement of the students, but it also applies to grown-ups who have yet to expand their awareness:

> The only people who can help these children get onto a track that shifts them out of the poverty cycle are the teachers who are able to make contact with them. With kindness, compassion, understanding, and most of all, instigating a sense of wonder. If they can ignite a child's curiosity, then they open up a channel that has thus far been closed or at least not used by them. And since it deals with the higher mind, it's significantly deeper than the survival-level connections that have been the child's life to date.

16 - No Bad Dreams

Love doesn't make the world go round.
Love is what makes the ride worthwhile.
– Franklin P. Jones

The immense volume of knowledge that was intrinsic in you when you arrived in this world was pushed to the back of your mind with information and training about how to take your place in today's society. Everything you knew when you were born has had little meaning to you. So how do you approach understanding your place in the world?

Maybe think of it this way. You have come into a movie late and you have to figure out the plot and the role of the characters in the story. Oh, and off screen, in real life, you are one of the characters, but you don't have a script. What makes it a real challenge is determining your individual role in this story that is your life.

That world that you learn to navigate has thousands of years of history, with the current narrative having been passed along through more than 500 generations, with the current social structure having been built off the bones of its predecessors. What was the same about each of the generations is that they were indoctrinated so completely that they had virtually no awareness of the far larger reality that had been indelibly papered over to induce full participation in the current set-up.

Actually, that's not quite true. We connect to that omniscient realm in our dreams. Hah! You knew they must be good for something. More than something. It's like "E.T. Call Home". We receive a tremendous amount of information in our asleep dreams, though most people haven't figured out how to relate to them.

The awake mind of the vast majority of people is set to default to the Ego's narrative. The asleep mind - the dream mind - defaults to the True Self. With the Ego default, we presume we understand what we are experiencing in dreams, but often we don't. With the True Self, we are always open afresh to what we perceive without presumption or prejudice.

> Higher consciousness enables us to go into the pre-conscious mind to alter the Ego default, to redirect the mind to be informed by the True Self. It largely depends on the history of the individual, and it takes a clear mind and quality intention to achieve this goal. As you can imag-

ine, shifting the default from Ego to True Self significantly upgrades the quality of your life.

To parse dreams, you must first understand that dreams come from a far more conscious energy system than the one we have been taught to understand. The language is different which is why it is so difficult to understand the messages that dreams can communicate. We receive input from the dream images that we only can presume that we (1) recognize and (2) understand.

Rarely do we get obvious messages in our dreams. So we interpret what we remember and almost always get it wrong. Often the interpretation is tainted by the hopes and fears we bring to the process of trying to figure out what the images and the themes mean. If we are cheerful, we view the dream as positive. If we are Pollyanna-ish, we see it as good as it can be. And if we are negatively inclined, we are likely to see it as a bad dream.

Whatever our interpretation, we are likely to be wrong in how we read the dream. And not just wrong, but we will be denying ourselves of the true meaning of it.

Second is that the language of our thoughts which we use to interpret our dreams (and our feelings) was probably created starting before we were born and inserted into an unsophisticated mind. And because the interpretation was so primitive when imbedded in the mind, it became very difficult to revise or update it.

And the third thing that you need to know - and the most important when it comes to interpreting dreams - is that there are *no bad dreams*. We've just been misinterpreting what we remember of the images we saw when we were asleep. Your mind has no intention to hurt, punish, or frighten you. That would be counterproductive to raising your consciousness.

> It must have been Christmas 1985, when I was living in a house perched on a cliff side in Big Sur. I woke up from a dream in which I was standing around with a small group of friends, and I had my hands around the throat of one of them. Harry was the name of the friend that I was strangling. It was not a violent scene. We were all quiet. Quiet because I was having no effect. I couldn't strangle him; I wasn't even hurting him. My friends were all just waiting for me to stop what I was doing. Which I did.
>
> Was it a good dream? I think so. Or rather, not good *per se* but informational, as all dreams are. My father's middle name was Harold. My interpretation all these years later is, Was the would-be strangler my Ego and Harry was my True Self, or was it vice versa?

Just as there are no bad dreams, there are *no good*

dreams either. All dreams are meant to be purely informative. So when you are mulling over what you think was a bad dream, stop and presume that you erred in your perception of what you think you visualized and remembered. Look at what made you feel negative about the dream, review those images, and come up with an at least neutral interpretation.

But really, until you reach a high level of consciousness, it's unlikely that you can do this since the perception and interpretation of the vast majority of dreams - good, bad and indifferent - are at best a misunderstood muddle of images and interpretations. Such confusion is often met with the popular toss-off, "Too bad life didn't come with a user's manual."

Actually it did. You just have to clear your mind of what you learned on arrival. Your original mind, the one you had when you were conceived, is supported by your True Self. But since you have learned to manage life here on Earth by creating a personality that operates as an interface between who you really are, and who you have decided to show yourself to the outside world, you haven't the mindset to begin to make use of the incredible information that dreams have to offer.

17 - Dark Moods and Ecstasy

Sometimes the road less traveled is less traveled for a reason. - Jerry Seinfeld

In his book *He: Understanding Masculine Psychology,* Robert A. Johnson wrote about how the dark male mood plays out, and also how a bad mood can be lifted. Most people believe that a bad mood must be suffered until it simply runs its course, so the fact that its duration can be brought up short is a big deal.

The first step to dissolving a bad mood is to figure out how and why it was teed up. What were the negative thoughts and/or feelings? What was the purpose of your mind putting you into a funk?

There are two likely answers to the first question. One is that you got some bad news that spoiled your day, and the other is that you have a generally negative outlook on life. So that even news that may not be particularly bad but is confusing or that leaves you in doubt, will take you under the dark cloud.

Also, a life without positive experiences will become unbalanced so that negative attitudes and expectations will create a foundation on which a dark mood can form.

There are several directions you can take to reduce the feeling of bad moods and to prevent them from taking hold. First, you need to realize that your mood is about something that has happened or that you are expecting to happen. If you get your mind back into the moment, you have a good place from which to focus on the issues that launched you into the mood.

Understand that bad moods come from judgments that a situation or conditions are dark. You can change your view about the circumstances that produce that judgment. Re-examine the elements and put them in a less hostile perspective. The range of that reassessment might extend from deciding there is nothing you can do about it so you can let go of it for the moment, to finding a specific solution to what it is that you found negative.

Another approach is to stand back and see the mood not as encompassing you but as a cloud over you, and thus you have the ability to lift it off of your mind. It might take some practice to see your True Self as separate from the dark cloud and not in it, but the more often you do it, the sooner the realization of the separation will come to you. And in that moment of separation, you will feel a sense of relief and of self-satisfaction that you can end the darkness. It is in that awareness that your mind will dispel the mood.

Of course there are various degrees of darkness and weight of moods, and it can take some time and serious concentration to get yourself in a place where you can free yourself. Factors can be reasons for the mood - there can be only one, but more often, there are several coalescing around the same time - and how long they have been on your mind before you were engulfed and responded.

But what you want to remember is that you have the facility of knowing that you can relieve yourself of this burden because you got into it. By staying with the effort to free yourself, by eschewing the justification you have given yourself that got you into the bad mood, along with some even breathing and maybe a slowly-poured glass of something, you can feel it dissolve away.

> An example of putting one's self into a bad mood is the bane of many journalists. We see so much bad news, so much awful behavior, so many clowns and cretins. The other evening, I had just read about Kyrsten Sinema, the Democratic Senator from Arizona who was threatening, not for the first time, to undermine an important piece of her party's legislation. It was very disturbing. It

put me in a dark cloud.

And then I realized how unnecessary it was for me to go there. After all, I couldn't do anything about it. She might in the end support the measure. And further, who knows if something better would come along as the result of her position. The dark cloud dissolved. I felt very pleased with having seen my negative pattern, and further, realizing that I all too frequently have subjected myself to such the unnecessary distress. From now on, I vowed, as much as I loved watching history being written, I would not take any of it personally.

Another benefit of removing the dark cloud is that it clears your mind and gives you a better view of the issues that brought on the mood. You also will be able to see the path you took to get into it, which will reveal waypoints that you might keep an eye out for the next time you might be feeling moody. So you can avoid the process in the future.

Some time ago, I saw in my behavior a pattern that I named *the precautionary mind*. It played out in my thinking as experiencing failure in advance of an impending situation. For instance, I would be having an interview for a new gig the next week, and I would experience the feeling of the effort failing now.

The concept being that if it did fail, I would have

> already felt bad about it, and if it went well, that would be great. While it made sense to consider what the results of not being successful would or could be, did I really have to feel the pain in advance? Once I realized the pattern, I moved quickly and successfully to end it.

* * * * *

Good moods certainly feel better and are, obviously, generated from positive experiences. They may be particularly welcome if you've recently climbed out from under a bad mood. So enjoy the good mood; bask in the light.

But know this. Good moods are also based on where you've been or where you are going. The more you are in the moment, the more you are balanced, the deeper you will feel better. That's because the highs which replaced the lows are a joy. You should certainly enjoy the good feelings, and by lowering the joy from peak levels to closer to Earth you'll be able to enjoy higher feelings longer.

And here is another reason to mitigate your exuberance. The definition of *ecstasy* is "an emotional or religious frenzy or trance-like state." It's from the Greek word *ekstasis* and means "standing outside one's self." To know when you feel ecstatic suggests that you will recognize what you are experiencing, and you will make that return to back inside yourself smoother.

18 - Who Am I?

Living at risk is jumping off the cliff and building your wings on the way down.
– Ray Bradbury

One afternoon, I needed to get away from my home situation. The woman I was living with and I needed some space apart. I was in Mill Valley. I started off heading north, but I changed my mind, turned around, and headed south. At some point I was driving down I-5 headed for Desert Hot Springs. When I was about an hour away, I was thinking about checking into a motel.

And then a strange question entered my mind: "Who am I going as?" In those exact words. I was startled at the question.

Who was the person who was going to stand before the counter at the motel and sign in? Not that the clerk would ask more than that I fill out the registration form and provide a credit card. But there was usually, naturally, chit-chat with the clerk at the desk, Where are you from? Where are you going? Well, I knew where I was coming from, but I didn't know where I was headed. And more personally, what I expected to come of this trip.

My internal discussion in the car was not wondering what I would say to the clerk, but what I was thinking about myself in that moment. And to be clear, I was not worried or distressed about my thoughts. I was taken aback by the conversation I was having with myself; in fact, I was actually energized. I didn't know the why of it all, but I knew it was significant. I'd never been here in my mind before. It was a step up the consciousness ladder, although I didn't know to see it as that at the time.

I can't say any more about the experience, except that it happened more than 35 years ago, and it has come to mind a good number of times to remind me that I haven't answered the question of who I am.

I'm not sure it matters, though it has come up in my dreams. I have more than a few times awakened from a dream in which there was a scene in which I was looking for one of my business cards to provide a person with my contact information. But as I went through my wallet, I shuffled through various cards that weren't mine, or were mine but were written on or dated, but never found a clean and correct card. Of course it had to do with something about identity. The failure to find the right card has come up in my dreams enough that I am aware of that fact in my dreams. Who am I? I'm not sure that there is an answer.

19 - In and of the World

If your head tells you one thing, and your heart tells you another, before you do anything, you should first decide whether you have a better head or a better heart. – Marilyn vos Savant

I was scouring the Internet for this phrase, *being in the world and of the world,* and I could not find the whole piece. I was going to leave it there, but then I was scrolling through my vast field of several dozens of pages of notes for this book, looking for something else, and Whoa, Nelly! I stopped the scroll. There was this line:

"IN the world and OF the world." - Sabrina.

It had been hiding from me in all my searches because there was no "being" in the line. But before I get into the exciting details of the discovery, a moment please on the discovery itself. Because this is something I talked about earlier. Recently, I have been able to find things by either moving my glance or getting a picture of where it is in my mind's eye.

The other way I find things is that I stop looking for them and suddenly there they are, and that's what happened here.

Now back to the plot of being of the world. It was from the 1954 film *Sabrina* with Humphrey Bogart and Audrey Hepburn; the words were in a letter she was writing to her father from Paris, where she had been sent to cooking school for two years, during which time her father hoped that she would forget her girl-age crush on William Holden.

This is part of what she wrote to her father: *I have learned how to live, how to be IN the world and OF the world, and not just to stand aside and watch. And I will never, never again run away from life. Or from love, either.*

As she indicated, being IN the world, you're reading the script. Being OF the world, you're writing the script. That is such a powerful statement of how we are going to live our lives. Are we satisfied with just being observers or role players? Or are we going to live full lives of quality, integrity, and purpose? That you are reading this book suggests that you have made the richer choice.

(References in the Appendix)

20 - Who Are We?

Some mathematician, I believe, has said that true pleasure lies not in the discovery of truth, but in the search for it. – Tolstoy

There are some very entertaining alternatives to learn about who we are other than reading Jung or similar complex treatises. But I'm thinking of watching certain movies. Like *The Wizard of Oz,* that came out in 1939. It was made from L. Frank Baum's children's fantasy novel called *The Wonderful Wizard of Oz,* written in 1900. It illuminated the American myth for much of the last century with the good witch and the bad witch, the characters representing intelligence, heart, and courage, and "There's no place like home."

Perhaps the most important character in the film was the dog, Toto. He was the *fifth business,* a role that is defined as neither the hero nor villain, but one that brings about the denouement. Consider that Toto caused Dorothy to run away because he reportedly bit Miss Gulch. He led Doro-

> thy's rescuers to the witch's castle. He pulled back the curtain to reveal the Wizard as a fake. And finally, going after another dog, Toto forced Dorothy to miss her balloon ride. That brought Glinda the Good Witch to help Dorothy and Toto to more suredly get home.

The American myth was updated when the first *Star Wars* film was released in 1977 (*A New Hope*). The boy becomes a man, the outlaw becomes a hero, the woman is not only a beautiful princess but also a serious warrioress, and Chewbacca. Plus there is a war between The Light and The Dark Side, and in the finale, technology is superseded by trust in the true self.

Myths are far more important than pure entertainment, but George Lucas' reach was stunning and has not gone away ... it was that powerful a message. The film has been a significant part of our society's identity for a half-century. If you doubt it, consider how the *Star War* characters have become ubiquitous in our culture.

And more important than any of the characters was *The Force*. It was a prime alternative to - and sometimes a replacement of - religion. It shifted the notion of many people from obeying an external god to a shared responsibility with *The Force*. From the time the film debuted until today, U.S. church membership has dropped by a third.

Energy and consciousness ... That's big stuff.

21 - *Creativity*

Use only that which works and take it from any place you can find it. – Bruce Lee

What is creativity? I asked Google that question and found, "the use of the imagination or original ideas, especially in the production of an artistic work; inventiveness imagination innovation originality individuality artistry expressiveness inspiration vision."

Imagination is undervalued and easily dismissed. It is far more than silly daydreaming. It is the mind producing larger and different ideas, from whole cloth or from multiple pieces of text, image, or sound; numbers or letters; new or old. You can have a picture of something in your mind only wanting for parts, or a palette of colors that only lack the eye to bring them beautifully together. That's where imagination comes in.

The first word that came to mind - my mind - about creativity was joy, and with that I thought that creativity also means being well-used. I was slightly off the definitional track, but that's what creativity means to me. It means thoughts, ideas, and words, appearing from somewhere deep and inducing me to type what I'm thinking as fast as I can, trying to keep up until the flow suddenly stops.

I have had a number of experiences of typing away, especially when writing fiction, when I looked up at what I had just written and saw something that had not crossed my mind. At least not my conscious mind. In one story I was writing dialogue between a couple - he's 62 and she's 32 - who were very much in love. Reluctantly he raises a concern about the age difference. She responds, saying that age doesn't matter. And then she says, "We owe no dues to the arithmetic of time."

That line never appeared in my conscious mind. I sat there looking at it, wondering who had written it. It seemed almost beyond my reach, but those words had indeed appeared on the screen because my fingers had struck the appurtenant keys.

The philosopher Shirley Luthman wrote, "No writer worth his salt can deny having sat down and taken dictation." She was so right.

> My first experience of taking dictation was when I was 15. I was going to the Smith College-Northampton High summer school five mornings a week, taking a history and a contemporary thea-

> tre course. On Monday of the final week, I had to turn in something I wrote for the theatre course. The day before, I sat down at my Smith Corona and banged out a nine-page story on that old yellow math paper about students at a prep school with a *Candid Camera* twist. I didn't reread it. I just handed it in the next morning. It won a $2 second prize.

Shirley and I had lunch with a mutual friend who had introduced me to her. This was 1983ish, decades before I had written that line. But I remember vividly a critical point in the conversation. She asked me if I had incorporated some of the concepts about which she had written and spoken about with me that had to do with higher consciousness. What she was referring to had been new to me, and while I was attracted to what she had laid out, I couldn't say that I had yet incorporated it at a level of full comprehension. She smiled at me and said, "You can't be on both sides." That's when I got it. I smiled at her with warmth and appreciation and nodded my head.

* * * * *

Creativity is best fostered in an open mind. The more you are able to clear your thoughts – especially repeated thoughts about what is past or in the future – the more room you have for new thoughts to appear. And they do. Some need to be quickly written down, at least enough words so you will be sure to recall the substance. And especially if you're in a situation where you can't immediately culture it because, for instance, you are writing about something else that requires serious attention.

Another facet of creativity is exemplified when I'm writing and a word comes to mind that I'm not familiar with; maybe I haven't used it before. So I think about alternatives, I'm not satisfied, and I look up the "new" word to discover it is exactly right for what I was writing. What is the old saw? Use a word three times and it's yours. But use it in writing you may lock it in because when you write it, you codify its existence with your fingers producing it and your eyes seeing it in context. Plus, you experience the satisfaction of having added to your vocabulary.

There is another value that invites creativity to your mind. It is the pleasure of sharing knowledge with others. Some people are showing off what they know, but the truly creative are purposed to gift another mind and enjoy the light of wisdom shining in his face.

* * * * *

I've also been shooting photographs since I was 12. Back in those days I loaded the film cartridges, developed the film, and printed the pictures. When I was 17, I shot 54 feature pix that were published in the Daily Hampshire Gazette, twelve of them in a couple of two-page displays. Capturing a person's character, an event, or a story in a still photograph is its own reward.

* * * * *

I don't know if everyone does this; I presume you do. It's saying something to myself, not necessarily aloud, but running it by me to see if it's sound, if it makes sense. If it would work if I said it aloud to someone. Would it catch the attention of an audience or readers?

What I find interesting about this is that there are two facets of my mind working together. My experience is that the listener provides an unequivocally honest review. There might be editing suggestions, but never a false compliment. So there is no question that the listener is the True Self.

I wonder if the speaker is the Ego. If so, it would certainly devolve some credit to the Ego for creativity; that it should certainly be heard in special cases - i.e., when it shows quality - and it should not be summarily silenced.

> Here's an example from a dozen years ago. I was walking along by the ocean as I did almost every day to clear my mind. I was doing some political consulting at the time, and my mind suddenly popped up a TV commercial for my client in a gubernatorial race.

> The video would start with a close up shot of a spoon dipping into a bowl of soup and bringing it to the mouth of someone yet unidentified. There was a voice-over, citing the problems that the people of the state, his would-be constituents, were facing. Then toward the end of script, the shot widened out to reveal the candidate eating the soup, and the voice-over was something like, "Soup is not enough for all that ails us. We need Tom Campbell."
>
> The spot never made it to the drawing board. I don't know if it would have changed any voters' minds but it certainly would have gotten some press.
>
> (If you don't know about Tom Campbell, let me tell you that he was one of the brightest, most authentic people I've met in all my years of covering government and politics. He has also been a valued friend.)

Anyway, I was pleased by how my mind worked. New ideas can't all be gems, but they can be worthy of reasoned interest. I would also note that ideas can sound good in one's mind, or spoken, and then lose their umph on paper or in video. But in the process, they can reveal not only fresh, creative ideas, but also a look into how the mind works. And some of those pieces can be cultivated again, with better results.

In another situation, I heard a story that I didn't know if it was true but which was interesting and made enough sense that I put it in a novel: "Let me tell you a story told to me by a doctor friend. He had a schizophrenic patient who was brought to the hospital with a blood sugar count of 500. That's very high. They were worried about how to treat her, thinking she might die. So she changed into her other personality, and the number dropped to normal."

A real doctor friend told me that he didn't know if that was possible, but he thought if the venue was changed - say, it was a high blood pressure issue - it could very likely pass muster.

Let me finish this bit by saying that history is filled with stories of brilliance that was delivered when the time wasn't right. Galileo promoted Copernicus' radical view that the Sun, not the Earth, was the center of the Universe. He was targeted by the Roman Inquisition for blaspheming the Holy Church and later spent the last years of his life under house arrest. But don't be deterred.

22 - What ... A Coincidence?

I've often noticed that once coincidences start happening they go on happening in the most extraordinary way. I dare say it's some natural law that we haven't found out.
– Agatha Christie

Years ago, I made a list of the favorite explanations people gave when they couldn't explain something. They attributed it to ...

God, capitalized or not;

Luck, good or bad;

Fate, so they're taking no responsibility;

Chance, a happenstance version of fate;

Accident, usually someone else's fault; and

Coincidence, really just an eponym.

Coincidence was my favorite because it strips the coterminous occurrence of the two events of all meaning.

Later, after moving to the west coast and slogging

my way into a higher level of thinking, I realized that the word needed new examination. Especially because I was having coincidental experiences that needed respect for what they really were. I did some researching and came upon some much deeper – or higher – thinking. Here were two lighter examples: Albert Einstein remarked, no doubt smiling, "Coincidence is God's way of remaining anonymous." And the philosopher G.K. Chesterton declared that "Coincidences are spiritual puns."

Over the years, having been witness to numerous coincidences that were too amazing to be written off so meaninglessly as coincidences, I came to reaffirm my awareness of the larger reality, that it was just beyond our vision of understanding. It was important, nonetheless, because not only did I see results of that larger reality, but the coincidences themselves also had significance.

The word I used for such coincidental events was synchronicity which one dictionary defines as, "the simultaneous occurrence of events which appear significantly related but have no discernible causal connection." A little bit dry but very much on point.

Then there is the warmer word, *serendipity*, that's used by people who are expressing some level of joy. Serendipity has some interesting roots. It's not clear – there are other explanations – but there is a reference to a Persian fairy tale from 1302 called *The*

Three Princes of Serendip. In that story, the clever princes "carefully observed their surroundings and then used their knowledge in ways that saved them from danger and death." So serendipity meant wisdom and chance in the same moment.

The word *coincidence* got its birth in American English when people learned that both Thomas Jefferson (our third president) and John Adams (our second president) died on July 4, 1826, fifty years from the day that they had signed the Declaration of Independence. John Quincy Adams (son of the second president and himself number six), called the coincidence of their deaths on the nation's anniversary "visible and palpable remarks of Divine Favor".

It was Carl Jung some 150 years later who came up with *synchronicity* which means "falling together in time." Simply put, it's a meaningful coincidence.

When I was looking up the distinction between synchronicity and serendipity, I found an interesting reference in *Psychology Today*. It noted right off that there are two schools of thought about coincidence - one is merely luck and the other is "meaningful, remarkable, and amazing." Yes, I'm an adherent of the second view.

> In his extraordinary book, *What's Bred in the Bone*, Robertson Davies presented this conversation:
>
> - Coincidence is a useful, dismissive word for people who cannot bear the idea of pattern shap-

ing their own lives.

- Coincidence is what they call pattern in which they cannot discern something they are prepared to accept as meaning.

With the realization that meaningful coincidences are sourced from the larger reality, I can look back over the years and recall dozens of such moments that occurred in my life, and all of them were significantly beneficial. First, I should note that some were just fun.

- I got on a plane in St. Thomas heading home to New York and seated next to me was a lovely woman who was to change planes there to fly home to Newport, Rhode Island. We had a marvelous time talking, getting to know each other, such that when we landed in New York, I rented us a car, drove to my apartment for some clothes, and then drove us up to Newport. It was the beginning of a delightful relationship.

- I was in an upscale bar in San Francisco with a friend. They had cups with five high-card poker dice in them on the bar. My friend shook his dice in the cup and poured them onto the bar. He had four kings. Wow. I shook my cup of dice and then put it open end down on the bar, concealing my dice.. "I won," I said with a confident smile. He didn't believe me of course and justly. How could I know? I lifted the cup off the dice. There were five aces.

There were a number of coincidences that were important.

- Back in 1971, I quit a $73/week copy boy job at ABC Network Television News to take a $200/week associate producer position at the New York public television station. The program was being produced by amateurs and I lasted all of three months. When I applied to return to the position at ABC, supported by the officials in charge of the division I had left, I was blocked by the corporate vice president for personnel with no explanation.

But as coincidence would have it, my grandfather played cards every evening with the same group of friends on the train from Grand Central Station to Mount Vernon where he lived. One of the people he played cards with every weekday was James Hagerty, who had served as the eighth White House Press Secretary under Eisenhower and then became a vice president of the ABC Network. I told my grandfather what had happened. He told Jim Hagerty. I got my job back two days later.

- When I was living in the Chicago area in the summer of 1992, between gigs, as they say, I was sitting on a chair in the waiting area in a state unemployment office. On the unoccupied chair next to me was a local paper, folded over to an inside page. I picked it up and saw that the owner of a software company had announced that he was running for Congress against Republican Representative Henry Hyde.

Hmm, I thought, and when I finished filling out forms at the unemployment center, I went home and called the fellow, Barry Watkins. I met with him the next day and was hired on the spot to manage his campaign. It wasn't a tough campaign; it was an impossible one. The district was heavily Republican and Hyde was a fixture.

But Barry and I had some fun. Do you remember Dan Quayle from his 1992 vice presidential campaign? He was at a school one day and he misspelled the word potato; he put an "e" on the end. He got a lot of press for it. Anyway, Barry had his people produce a piece of software called *The Unauthorized Dan Quayle Spelling Checker*. (This was 30 years ago so it came out on a 5¼ floppy disk.) Because the district was so Republican, Barry's campaign got very little attention. The public television station even got his name wrong. But went the ballots were counted, Barry got 35% of the vote which was considerably more than had been predicted. And Barry continues to be a friend many years later.

I want to reinforce that when you are on the right

track in your life, and your mind is open, what comes to you is beneficial, though sometimes it takes a second look to see it that way. Here is an example of a reordering of events that happened the day I finished writing the first draft of this book.

> This past Monday I had set up lunch with Patricia for Thursday. On Wednesday I set up breakfast with Gerard for Friday. Gerard called me later that day to say that he would be flying back to Chicago on Friday, and could we make our breakfast on Thursday instead. I said yes, that would be fine. I would have preferred not to have two meals out the same day because I would eat too much, but he is a best friend and leaving town. Later that day, Patricia called to see if we could make our lunch on Friday instead. Well, sure.

It was not a big deal, certainly, but it made my life easier, and I saw it as a note of recognition from the larger reality that I was on track in my work on this book.

23 - A Sixth Sense

Life is what happens to you while you're busy making other plans. – John Lennon

The sixth sense – also referred to as prescience, clairvoyance, second sight, foresight, divination, ESP – is very real. While it is defined simply as knowing something will happen before it happens, what happens or how it happens is not usually clear. Some adherents insist it's only people outside the paranormal that can't see what's coming. But maybe that's simply due to our narrow view of what is normal. The sixth sense is certainly more than a parlor game or a trick, as people who have experienced it will tell you. And I have.

Is there an explanation? Well of course there is. But it is not something you believe or have faith in. It is something you know; you think *It* and you feel *It*. You have experienced *It*.

If you're like me, you resisted accepting the notion of the sixth sense for the longest time. But then I had experiences that stretched the scientific *explanations* beyond reasonable bounds. Here are a few of the events that pushed my limits.

- I was sitting with my friend Joan in the living room of our house on the top of a cliff in Big Sur, talking about the clock on the wall above the sink in the kitchen. The minute hand was attached only by a small piece of duct tape, which, while efficient, was hardly aesthetic. My thought was that I should remove the minute hand because we didn't need it, since we were staying around the house most of the time, and we could always guess the time within a few minutes by the position of the hour hand. A minute later I got up to get a glass of water. I walked across the unyielding stone floor to the kitchen where, when I was a few feet from the sink beneath the clock, the minute hand fell onto the counter.

- Another instance took place on Highway One along the Mendocino coast, late on a Tuesday afternoon, with no other cars on the road for minutes at a time. I was telling my friend Rita about a National Endowment for the Arts funding issue, and how there was a brouhaha over a grant to an obscure performance artist who had been receiving taxpayer money to support an act which included urinating on stage on a picture of Christ. At that very moment, we came around a curve in the road, and there was a man urinating into the bushes. He had parked his car on the other side of the road, walked across to our side for no obvious reason, and was relieving himself in full view.

- An old college friend I hadn't spoken with in fifteen years - and haven't spoken to since - called me one evening just to say hello. In the course of the conversation, she mentioned her great pleasure in reading a science fiction writer named John Varley. I'd never heard of Varley, but that wasn't surprising since sci-fi wasn't a great interest of mine. After we had talked for over a half-hour, I returned to watching a videotape. When the tape ended and I turned the player to rewind, the television reverted to channel three, the station behind the tape player. On the television channel, they were showing the opening credits of a movie, and the first credit I saw said it was based on a short story by John Varley.

- A few years ago, while working on a book for a client, I decided to speak of what I referred to as the larger reality, as *The Force*, as everyone would understand the reference. That afternoon, when I was out walking the dog, a van drove past me, and across its back window was a large-letter decal that read, "May The Force Be With You".

And I would add this experience from my friend, Barry, the Congressional candidate:

> – A number of years earlier, when Barry was in England, he got a call from Chicago. Barry said he knew as he lifted the phone from the cradle that his father had died. How? I asked. I don't know, he said. He couldn't call it just a coincidence, but he refused to entertain speculation about anything intangible.

Most people have had similar if less dramatic experiences, or have heard personal accounts from otherwise-trustworthy friends, of people simultaneously knowing of the death of someone hundreds or thousands of miles away.

In regards to my experiences, is *extraordinary coincidence* enough to explain such incidents? Or is there something connecting us that we aren't, for the most part, consciously aware of? I pick door number two.

24 - *Validation*

People who think they know everything are a great annoyance to those of us who do.
– Isaac Asimov

Maybe because much of my professional life in broadcasting required being tight with time, I have always kept a keen eye on the clock. It has meant that I am always on time or early, and often impatient with others who are late. What is interesting to me lately about the time are the numbers themselves. Especially when I check the time and it is something like 2:22, 4:44, or 5:55. Or what I just noticed on the digital display in the bottom right-hand corner of my screen, which has the date and a six-digit clock. It read 6/22 02:22.22. Once when I looked at my watch it read 12:34:56.

These might seem amusingly unimportant, but they are meaningful to me. I have defined them as so. I smile when I see those readings. Because I never make an effect to see such a time, nor do I look again to see it when it is soon to occur. That would be cheating.

In one day, looking at three different clocks I saw 5:55, 3:33, and 4:44. It turned out to be a very good day for me.

My favorite is 11:11.

Let me describe it in a different way. Of course it is coincidental, and it is my creation. The clock happens to be displaying a numerically-special time when I happen to look at it. For me, it's about being in sync with the larger reality. It's a confirmation of the relationship.

There are other occurrences that are acknowledgments of the relationship with the larger reality. I don't like to handwrite because to keep up with my thoughts, I usually write too fast and it later takes time to read my rather messy writing, whereas I can type very quickly and keep up with my thoughts. But sometimes my computer will be off and I will need to write. I pick up a pen and I can write a full page of something that is on my mind. It underlines this as a special event – I'm in the groove, so to say – reaffirmed by the fact that the handwriting is particularly readable, and the text clean and needing very little editing. That means a lot, but maybe only to a writer. This reminds me of what Saul Bellow observed, "You never have to change anything you got up in the middle of the night to write."

Another connector, if you will, is that I might be

looking for something, for instance a book that could be in several places. Often I will look up and find I'm looking right at it, or I'll have an image in my mind's eye of where it is.

The mind's eye is extraordinary. There have been numerous occasions when I have tried to remember a name or a word, and I will suddenly see it written in my mind's eye. It's always in block letters and it disappears as soon as I say the name or word silently in my conscious mind.

I have also learned that if I struggle to remember something, it will take a long while to remember it if it comes to my mind at all. So now I let go of the search almost immediately after I start it, and usually get the answer soon after I stop searching.

Another example of my mind working out of sight is that I have several times at the end of a long walk, my thoughts elsewhere, suddenly looked up to see that I have stopped where I parked my car ... when I was ready to walk by it. Probably it came into my vision, but I wasn't consciously looking for it. However, another part of my mind noticed it and notified me.

* * * * *

There are two games that I play to see if I am in synch with the larger reality in the moment. Sometimes when I am making scrambled eggs for Judy's breakfast, I take the cover off the sink drain and from several feet away I toss the shells into the drain. Well, sometimes they don't go in. (Alas, I had to stop the fun when the town said it was better for the sewage system if instead the shells were put in the garbage.)

The other game is when I finish my shower. I give the edge of the outer sliding shower door a little push to send it down the track next to the inner door. My aim is to have the shower door arrive precisely at the end of the track without bouncing back. Okay, it isn't an Olympic sport, but the better my touch, the more pleased I am in facing the day.

And there's this ... I used to work on *New York Times* Sunday crossword puzzles in bed before I went to sleep. When I got stuck, unable to answer a half-dozen clues, I'd close the book and turn out the light. The next night, I would usually know the answers to all or most of the missing answers. Clearly my mind was working while I was sleeping.

(I was just about to take a break and heat up a cup of coffee. I had figured out that if I only fill my cup to a certain level and I set the nuker to a minute-eleven (1:11) it heats it just right. Before I got up for my coffee break, I checked what page I was on. It was page 111.)

* * * * *

Sometimes I feel that a small part of me is out of sync, though in what way I'm not sure. But as I spend probably 60 hours a week at my desk, and have everything I use where I want it, if something is out of place I know it and I try to do something about it. In this case, I moved a clock from my adjoining second desk five feet away to my left. I relocated it to the left front corner of my desk. Now all I had to do to see the clock was to move my gaze a couple of feet from my monitor to the clock.

But something was not in sync. Every time I looked to see what time it was, I turned my head back to where the clock used to be. For three weeks, I made a serious effort to retrain myself to look at the clock in its new spot, but I finally gave up.

I moved a few small things around on the other desk and returned the clock to its original spot. Since then, I have without any thought, turned my head 30 degrees to see the clock. It's easy and it's perfectly comfortable. It's certainly not earthshaking, but I find it curious that I seemed unable to program my mind to see the clock in the place which didn't take moving my head, just my glance.

25 - *The Evolution of the Mind*

Once we accept our limits, we go beyond them.
- Albert Einstein

A very dear friend whom I think of as one of the brightest people on the planet has something of a blind spot. A scientist, she believes in the tangible, the physical. She speaks of the brain growing at a much slower pace than evolution. I am not concerned with the size of the brain because, as noted earlier, I see the brain as the hardware and the mind as the software. While the brain will grow only somewhat as we evolve, the mind is virtually limitless in the scope of how it can serve us.

One of the reasons ascribed to the break between Freud and Jung was Freud's belief that a person's unconscious mind is limited to his own experiences, while Jung said that a person's collective unconscious was not limited to his own experience but included the archetypes or imagery of human life from the beginning.

In his groundbreaking 1976 book, *The Origin of Consciousness in the Breakdown of the Bicameral Mind*, (what a great title) updated in 1990, Julian Jaynes wrote that human consciousness did not come into form until the 2nd century BCE, when human beings evolved to a level that they could use language to store and access thoughts in their mind. He said that prior to gaining consciousness, the bicameral mind operated with verbal hallucinations, and that consciousness dramatically opened up the realms of imagination and memory, and the ability to understand thoughts and feelings.

We come into this life with access to all the information in the human universe. It's not that we have it all memorized. Rather, we can seek it and with the right frame of mind, retrieve it. (In the Appendix is more about people accessing a higher level of consciousness.) The reason why we don't know how to do it innately is that we did until it was taught out of us.

The first thing a human being is cognizant of in his early days is existence. Mostly that is experiencing his immediate physical environment in terms of need and discomfort. Hunger, needing to be burped, dirty diapers changed, it being too hot or too cold, lights too bright, sounds too loud, and otherwise being physically uncomfortable - those are the essentials of early life. Then he develops a maturing awareness of input to his five senses: sight, sound, smell, taste, and touch. And after a while there's awareness of a difference between his being and what is not his being. It is then that he begins to develop an interface with everything that is not himself but Other.

He figures out what it takes to get his vital needs met, as in to be fed and changed. Mostly he has depended on his providers to know what he requires, but soon he learns to communicate his needs in very basic terms; for instance, crying generates attention. And he realizes that giggling and smiling generates approbation. Now he's on his way to full-scale manipulation of his environment.

This is where the use of the mind begins to become important. There is a massive amount of information to take in, parse, and understand, though most of it comes through the parents and siblings. Plus the new child has to learn about babysitters and other regular participants in his early life. Most of it is absorbed and categorized according to very simple cause-and-effect charting. If he does this, that happens, and interestingly, at a very early age, he is not just learning but teaching. For instance, what works to get mom to change him might have to be tweaked in some way, perhaps urgently, when mom isn't there; how to tell someone unfamiliar with his signals to get the job done.

This is a critical stage in building consciousness because it requires the infant to realize that not everyone understands the same signals in his repertoire. From this point on, nuance becomes a vital issue for him with the realization that every human being is different; to be listened to and spoken to differently. This understanding is made deep down, but what to do about it is registered and programmed in his mind ... The Ultimate App.

26 - Who's There?

The wisest man is he who does not fancy that he is so at all. – Nicolas Boileau-Despr

As noted previously, there's a big difference been looking and seeing. When you look, you're searching and your vision is focused and thus limited. When you are seeing, you are open to what earns your attention.

Recently I've found that I can see in a person if they are truly conscious. This is because rather than looking at their eyes or mouth or expression or pose, I'm taking in their whole being and I can tell if they are self-aware. If their energy shows them to be open and thoughtful. If they are coming from their True Self, not their Ego.

I think coupled with these troubled times there is growing awareness of the larger reality, and it is logical for people of higher consciousness to more easily recognize each other.

It is said that the eyes are the window to the soul.

What you see in someone's eyes is also how they see you. It's more than an image. In the eyes of a conscious person, you can see acceptance.

I believe that we are born with the ability to see auras which indicate a person's character and integrity. But that was something that was taught out of us. "No my dear, that man doesn't have an indigo halo."

Here is an excerpt from *Just Imagine,* a novel about auras that I wrote in 2011:

> I myself don't believe in a white-robed, white-bearded, god dispensing iconic justice, but I'm quite aware that there is some ontological force in the universe that is running things. I believe that it becomes more visible to us as we increase our consciousness, and that it will become ever more obvious, particularly to those who value higher consciousness, in the coming years.
>
> Most who have beliefs in gods of any religion will eventually evolve to a point that, because of what they experience, will shift their thinking from a belief in an external deity to the recognition of an individual godhood within each of us. Instead of listening to the drone of preachers, they will know some version of the Christ Consciousness deep in their own souls.
>
> Auras are about consciousness, and consciousness is different from book-larnin'. It has to do

with an open mind and an open heart. It's not about academic degrees or large bank accounts.

Consciousness is a quality of the expanded human mind. Though it has always been with us, it only recently has caught on in a big way among a growing segment of the population. Back in ancient times, the most conscious person in the clan or tribe was often the shaman or the witch doctor. Later they became the important philosophers. They also were likely the "witches" in Europe and in Salem, Massachusetts, who were slaughtered by those who felt their own crude, mindless power being challenged.

Auras enable us to recognize the level of peoples' consciousness.

The ability to see auras will greatly divide the people on our Earth between those who are of lower consciousness and willing to stay down there - usually in fear or anger - and those who are habitually seeking to expand their awareness. It is my guess that when it comes to thinning the human herd, as we might expect will happen in the not-too-distant future, it will be on the basis of consciousness.

I have no idea how that will happen, though a plague weeding out the unconscious isn't a bad bet. Surely we will want the finest minds on our planet to be the ones to build a new global community, and all that that entails.

Now instead of auras we can perceive a person's character with soft mind, as discussed in Chapter *11 - On the Mat.*

As we can certainly get a sense of who people from their posture, how they speak, and what they say, and since the person's energy is what produces all those indicators, we can very likely find that we can sense a person's energy picture just by being with them rather than looking for individual signs.

27 - *Judgment*

What power has love but forgiveness?
– William Carlos Williams

Abraham Lincoln said, "If you look for the bad in people expecting to find it, you surely will." That underscores how easy it is to form a judgment. Easy? Judgments are formed virtually effortlessly. They come about when you encounter someone who is, in your judgment, misbehaving in some way.

Or not even doing something wrong. Consider how quick we are to feel defensive when we encounter someone who is only marginally familiar with our language. Think of your last call for tech support . Very easy.

But there is a cost. As Eldridge Cleaver observed in *Soul on Ice,* "The price of hating someone is loving one's self less."

Judgments are easier to make than to edit, erase, or reverse. It is not easy to admit to ourselves that we were wrong, about anything. Even when confronted with evidence that a decision was wrong, we are often slow to acknowledge it. What happens when you run into some past offender sometime later, and he apologizes to you for his past behavior, explaining that he was on some new meds that disoriented him? Maybe you will clean his entry or note it with an asterisk.

Making judgments - good and bad - get in the way of clear thinking. All judgments are detrimental in that you are tying yourself to the past. Of course you have your experiences which naturally have emotional flavors to them. But the less that you lock them in, the more you put them somewhat aside in a new encounter, the more open you will be to the possibility that you misread the previous misbehavior. You will feel better about yourself even if the situation reveals that the earlier offender hasn't changed his feathers.

How confusing it is when someone you have judged to be stupid does something brilliant. Or when someone you don't like does something praiseworthy. Why should you put yourself through the cumbersome process of revising your opinion of the person to recognize the value of their deed? If you have already let go of your judgment, or lessened your grasp on it, the decision is easier to drop or edit.

The issue of judgments comes down to this : If you

don't make judgments, you are less encumbered in your thinking today. You can decide in the moment the true value or integrity of a person, an idea, or an action. So don't waste your mind judging.

* * * * *

We all too often confuse behavior with the individual. Think of the clarion call from the Christ Consciousness that we all too often appear to forget: "Love the sinner, hate the sin." If you take the position that behavior is only one act in a life-long play, you - the observer - can give people the room to grow and regret. And there is the incumbent value that you experience less anger and less fear.

> I used to describe some of my feelings of anger as righteous. I don't recall ever having a label for the non-righteous version. But at some point, I thought the notion of righteous anger was giving myself justified permission to be anger. How dumb. That was then that I stopped using the term. When writing this bit, I looked up the term "righteous anger" I discovered that it means "being angry at all the things that oppose God." That seems rather limiting.

Yes, I know this calls for a huge realignment. Letting go of making judgments is a challenge because we have been raised to make immediate decisions about most people and situations we encounter. It's a foundational precept of our fight-or-flight indoctrination dealing with people or situations we consider a real or potential treat. But we have an opportunity when we realize that we have made a judgment to release it in that moment. It is most worthwhile because doing so is likely to produce a strong sense of satisfaction at releasing someone from a needless negative hold.

All this said, there is nothing to suggest that you will forget the behavior that you found wrong - or good - at the time. Likely it was. So what? Now is another time. He may have been having an unusually bad day then or he simply misunderstood the situation. And maybe he regretted it the minute you had left. Or it could be you that was the offender.

Another point. You are not the only beneficiary of dissolving a judgment. When you vow to meet everyone, known and unknown, with a fresh attitude you may be opening the door they need to move forward.

I know, I know, what I suggest sounds impossible. I haven't gotten there yet, not nearly. Maybe it's unattainable. But it's a reasonable goal, and my definition of *perfection* is that it *is the act of perfecting*.

Where to start? Instead of holding onto things that you find irksome in someone's behavior or character, adjust your view to see only the things that you love or respect about them and take them to heart.

I have mentioned previously that while working

on this book, I have experienced interventions that are significant to what I'm writing. This just happened again. There was a notification of a new email arriving in the inbox. It was from someone I had decided months ago was somewhat annoying. Not a bad person but someone who insistently arguing with the facts.

Bam! What I had just written got me between the eyes. Yes, I vowed that I would not crinkle up my attitude when I saw her name in my inbox again. All I need is love, right? And laughter at myself.

28 - *Woof! Woof!*

> *You can't be suspicious of a tree, or accuse a bird or a squirrel of subversion or challenge the ideology of a violet. – Hal Borland*

There's a bumper sticker that reads "Wife and dog missing. Reward for dog." Funny, well, for most people with any sense of humor, but there's also considerable truth in it. Because animals in our lives, treated well, return unconditional love. We find that so unlike so many people. That's why it's reported that having a dog can add ten years to your life. And not just dogs but cats and horses, and many other animals. Even some cold-blooded creatures as well; they seem to have warm hearts for the right people.

It's why there are programs to put animals, privately-owned and from organizations like the SPCA, in hospitals and homes for the elderly.

> The airlines were swamped by "support" animals of every variety, brought on planes by

> people who said they were dependent on them.
>
> A number of these cases, particularly those for war veterans, were legitimate. This was a relatively new phenomenon that got considerably out of hand. Some people would lie about the need to have a small animal with them, so they didn't have to pay to ship them. Considering the hassle that the untrained animals - human and otherwise - frequently caused on planes, most such people should have to bring a comfort person with them or take a bus.

But getting back to the real issue of loving a pet, if you've had the experience, you know that there is considerable communication experienced with the animal. My dog can tell when my mood is dark or sorrowful and she comes up close to me. Not only is she present, but she has a particularly caring expression on her face.

I report this about animals because there is so much about their energy that is similar to what human beings experience and exchange. You've likely heard stories about animals traveling hundreds of miles on their own, finding their way back to their owners. I read stories about a dog that rescued a woman from a car wreck about to explode, and a rabbit that woke a woman whose house was on fire by jumping up and down on her chest. There are also myriad photographs of different kinds of animals snugging together. They seem, in these cases, far less inhibited than people.

We should take note and try to be more open to the messages that we receive from other people. The information is there, but we are usually closed down to people we don't know or resist connecting with for various reasons. What it illuminates is that while we know that we are safe to express ourselves to animals, we are often reticent to speak to other people from our True Self without anticipating - correctly or not - their response.

Along with *Homo sapiens* becoming more sapient - well, some of them - I've noticed that dogs seem to be more evolved. My relationships with many animals, but dogs in particular, are enhanced. I've found more and better contact with animals I know and those that are new to me. I imagine that it is because I am coming directly from my True Self. I'm engaging them "personally" and not as just another animal. Maybe it's like they can hear dog whistles that humans can't, they seem to be able to sense a person's character. (Maybe they'll soon be sending us d-mail.)

To be clear, this is not just about dogs. I've had close relations with a few cats. And certainly many people find horses to be important friends.

But that's not my whole story. Much of my understanding of our connection with animals has blossomed over the last twenty years. Back then, when I lived in the wilds of northern California, ten miles outside of Redding, I had three encounters with rattlesnakes close to the house. I dispatched them safely - safe for me, terminal for them - and subsequently I have felt regret for killing them so easily. Yes, they were very close to the house, but they didn't directly threaten me at the time. However, they weren't the only rattlesnakes close by; one came from under the front deck, where it and others had found shade. (It got up to 118 degrees there every summer.) Buster, our dog, had once been bitten by a rattlesnake, but being over 100 pounds and bitten on a paw, he survived without noticeable damage. I sound like I'm making excuses for killing the snakes. My mind worked differently then.

* * * * *

Buster was my then-wife's dog, and he and I got along famously during my five-plus years there. He was probably 14 when it was time for me to move back to civilization. I wound up leaving on the Wednesday before Thanksgiving. My only real regret in moving back to Mill Valley was that I was leaving Buster. I said good-bye to him with love and appreciation; but he knew our time together was over.

Buster was old and failing. He had waited for me to come back after three weeks from where I was making new living arrangements to say good-bye.

The following Sunday, he relieved himself all over the living room, possibly as a message to my wife for not fixing what had been wrong between us. The next day he was ready to go, and he was taken to the vet to be put down. To this day, when I think of Buster, it is with deep gratitude.

* * * * *

A year or so later, I was at a friend's New Year's party. She had a four-foot corn snake house pet. Corn snakes aren't dangerous to human beings. But I learned more than that when my friend gently laid Tess in my lap. It took but a moment for me to restore my composure, and in another minute or so I started to feel Tess' energy. I began to gently stroke her and soon felt more than a snake in my lap. There was the sense of a live creature, as I would feel from and for a cat or a dog.

* * * * *

At this writing, I've been living with Gracie, a ten-year-old, twelve-pound Havanese-Maltese dog for six years and I owe her a good deal for my enhanced peace of mind. With her love and patience, she has taught me much. Like not to yell at her when she is barking. On one of my walks, the thought came to me that pets are angels that have come to Earth to show people how to feel love and to give love.

If people had tails like dogs, tails that would perform the same purpose of displaying pleasure with another beings, we would have a more peaceful world.

29 - *Relaxxx*

> *True knowledge exists in knowing that you know nothing, and in knowing that you know nothing, that makes you smartest of all.*
>
> *- Socrates*

Knowing how to relax is very important, but taking yourself away from what you were doing that is calling for you to relax is often something of a challenge. Maybe you're on deadline, or you don't like what you're working on and you want to get it over with. Those are often the best times to take a break. Even if it's just a short one.

Doing something very different like stepping away from the keyboard and doing the laundry or washing your car can be a good choice - a clean get-away, so to say. Another choice is something creative like preparing dinner. What you want is something that requires you to use different physical and mental processes. That said, I have sometimes switched away from working on a piece of writing to reading emails or checking news sites for the latest stories.

Going for walks, rolling shoulder muscles, smelling the roses ... there are all sorts of ways to relax, many that fit you personally, in different situations.

Your mind is calling your attention to the fact that you are in some sort of rut, and you need to take your attention elsewhere. This can sometimes be a challenge because while you are reaching for a deeper, quieter place in your mind, it can threaten the Ego's purported domination. Tell your task-master to take a hike.

> I found a healthful exercise in how to walk. Many men walk from their shoulders. I was walking from my hips. As a simple exercise, I started paying attention to feeling the energy reaching from my hips to my toes. Hips, thighs, knees, calves, feet. Very simple, it only required some attention ... when I remembered that I wanted to do it. Now it's normal, and it really feels wonderful.

* * * * *

There have been times when I am waking up but not yet fully awake that I have felt my Ego griping away at me. I could bè thinking about a problem I would be facing that day, and it would be presented as disproportionally large and/or difficult compared to what I really faced. And when I pushed that one away, another problem would surface, and then another. It was like a cloud of insects.

Ultimately I found the solution was to quiet my mind by first lightly flexing my muscles and then concentrating on slowing breathing. I would extend the peaceful feelings to my heart and lungs. This works because going physical provides a way to break the hold of the negative thoughts. I might also add counting down from 20 very slowly, so slowly that my mind would get distracted from the count-down, at which point I would start the count over again. Curiously, I found that also helped me to get back to sleep.

Sometimes when I didn't think that was going to do the job, and I was feeling more fully awake, I would turn on a light and read from a current book by my bedside - always keep a couple of books by your bed - until my mind was refocused from my issues to the pages. It was usually not much later that my eyelids began to feel heavy. And then with a smile of approval at my successful efforts, I would put the book down, turn off the light, and go back to sleep.

Of course if I found myself seriously awake, and I'd had enough sleep, it was time to get up and engage the day. And I did so in a far better mood.

Don't worry. Be happy. It's more than a jingle. Be in the moment. Be now. When you're working with your mind, it's the only place to be.

30 - Don't Think Before You Speak

If you could say it in words there would be no reason to paint. - Edward Hopper

Many people think before they speak, which makes some sense when you are addressing an audience in a formal situation. But otherwise, you can usually speak without a script, actual or virtual, just speaking from the thoughts that come to mind.

What is the source of those thoughts that are turned into the words you say? Yes, it is some part of your mind, if not the same part that contemplates what you want to say. So what is it then that determines the substance, the style, and the words?

There are two sources of our spoken words - our Ego and our True Self - that feed that part of the mind that produces speech, and from which it flows to the brain that actually pronounces what the mind decides we are to say.

A dozen years ago, I was the luncheon speaker at a political women's organization. There were maybe a hundred people in the room. I had notes to speak from for the allotted 20 minutes. At some point I stepped out from behind the podium, without my notes, and spoke off the cuff for the rest of an hour. I think only two people left the room before I'd finished.

There have been similar "work" situations where I spoke without thinking first about what I was going to - or wanted to - say. And increasingly, I've found that I'm listening better to what the person or people I'm with are saying - and subconsciously picking up their visual cues - to generate what I have to say.

I have recently had two significant examples of my True Self speaking without my thinking, these in personal situations. The first was with my very dear friend and colleague, Roger. He has a fine mind and is an important thinker and an excellent writer. He and I were on the phone talking about a new book he was writing. I made a suggestion to him about his approach to how he was writing it. He was struggling with the introduction. Without thinking what I was about to say, I told him to let go of the introduction and write the body first. Then he could come back and write the introduction. He would find it easier because he would know better what he was introducing. He thought that was fine idea. But to reiterate, that suggestion never appeared in my conscious mind. It just came out, but from where I don't know.

The other instance, I think it was the day after my phone conversation with Roger, was another telephone conversation during which a friend told me about her husband of more than 20 years announcing that he was moving to another state, and she wasn't coming with him. She didn't mind much not going with him as they hadn't been happy together for a long time, but he was also expecting her to support him ... as she had most of their marriage.

She tried to hold back her tears telling me this, but they came anyway. She said that she didn't want to cry on the phone with me. I told her, again without conscious thought, that the tears were the loosening up of the knots of tension she had tied up inside of herself over the years during their difficult times together. Apparently I was spot on because she immediately relaxed. She asked me how I knew that. I told her that's what tears are for, to let go of the pain.

In fact, I had never before read, said, heard, or even thought about the idea that tears were to loosen knots of tension that had been tied up inside someone.

I found both experiences validating.

* * * * *

My friend Roger has a sharp ear. He heard his seven-year-old nephew and the boy's six-year-old brother talking in a way that caught his breath.

"Are you forgetting?" the older boy asked.

"Yes, my *unitivity* to the Universe," his younger brother replied. (His word; meaning connection.)

Roger knew the boys to be particularly bright and thoughtful. And he knew from those words and other conversations they had had with each other and with him that they were born with more awareness of the collective unconscious. Roger and I have talked about such things over the years, and what he heard from the boys didn't surprise him so much as it reinforced how bright his nephews were. He shared their regret at losing what they had known, knowledge of their experience of a different, brighter time.

31 - *All the World's Players*

I own that I cannot see as plainly as others do, and as I should wish to do, evidence of design and beneficence on all sides of us. There seems to me too much misery in the world.

– Charles Darwin

William Shakespeare's sparkling "All the world's a stage" speech leads off with, *All the world's a stage, And all the men and women merely players.*

It goes on to note that, *They have their exits and their entrances,* and then speaks to the seven ages of life, from infant to, *Sans teeth, sans eyes, sans taste, sans everything.*

What struck me as I recalled the beginning words was that we are all dealing with those men and women whose paths we cross on the stage, basically as the character who they are playing. I mean, naturally, of course, but rarely do we see them for who they really are. And those characters that they are playing in their daily lives were fashioned during their early years of existence as they developed the Ego with which to manage their life.

Consider the vast amount of programming from their parents that took place in their first years, as their new beingness learned how to relate to the world. Probably 90% of the basics of life management - the personality, as it were - is formed by age five in a reasonably healthy home, and from then on there is tweaking to deal with the exigencies of life. Much of that tweaking was still fashioned with direction from the parents, and also input from teachers, siblings and other family, friends, and strangers.

What is critical to remember, often in the moment, is that the human being you are speaking with is a player who has been working with a script that was principally written with his parents whose own script was principally written for them by their parents and back down the line.

Such learning has two inherent flaws. One is that the personality, or Ego, takes evermore dominant control, which condemns the person to a negative default of anxiety and confusion. And second, by definition, it squelches any real chance of consciousness growing beyond basic levels

This has been showing in the socio-intellectual regression, particularly obvious to us in the United States and Western Europe. To wit, there is the inability to deal with climate change as the weather gets more violent more frequently, as government fails to move us away from fossil fuels. They also aren't doing anything about the lethal crisis of firearms. Other problems include the denial of women's reproductive rights, the growing restriction of voters' rights, and the collapse of public school education. There is also the refusal of tens of millions of people to get vaccinated against COVID. And perhaps most disturbing are the tens of millions of Americans who have continued to buy the lies of Donald Trump.

I suggested two years ago that we were dealing with a plague of insanity. That would explain much of the social disorder and the tacit acceptance of the corruption and incompetence of the management of our nation at national, state, and local levels, with few exceptions.

Back in the 1950s, John Calhoun conducted experiments with rats to determine what would happen when their population grew too large for its enclosure. What happened was that the rats went insane. They failed to bring fetal rats to birth, they stopped eating, and otherwise refused to keep themselves alive. The phase "Too many rats in the box" came from his experiments. That may be what is happening with human beings, with overpopulation now up to six billion people. We don't have the private time we need, nor enough space, enough quiet, or peace of mind. Many people are going literally crazy.

But curiously, or maybe not, with so much looking dark, there appears to be a considerable rise in individual consciousness. And this at a time when religiously-unaffiliated Americans make up a full 29% percent of the U.S. population; that's up 53% in ten years. Imagine a division between the haves and have-nots when it comes to awareness and the valuing of character and truth.

32- Higher Consciousness Glows

Truth is always exciting. Speak it, then. Life is dull without it . – Pearl S. Buck

I can tell you from personal experience that when I received my second vaccination, within minutes I started to feel better. More relaxed but more present and aware. I also felt less hurried, which showed in my driving. I didn't drive as fast as I used to. Not that I was aggressive on the road before, but after the second vaccination, I for some reason, didn't feel the same pressure to get to where I was going.

There were other signs of change. I didn't get annoyed as easily as I used to. And I found myself listening more rather than having to jump in with what I had to say. And my thinking was clearer. It wasn't as cut and dry; there was more subtlety and nuance ... more detail. My mind was open to considering more possibilities.

I also found that in my conversations with people I knew, I was not taking them for granted. I looked at them on every occasion with a fresh mind. And I was delighted to discover that I was seeing a new person; more thoughtful, more complex, more interesting, more valuable. And in their response to me I could see that they found me more interesting, more of a pleasure to be with. The exchanges were so significant that my friends were asking me if everything was all right. That I seemed changed.

The differences were more than noteworthy. I had never experienced myself this way, and I wondered what had caused the change. I was certainly aware that it had begun just after my second inoculation. I remembered having a quality conversation with the nurse who gave me the shot. It was not just off-the-cuff, it was substantial. We both valued the exchange, for the words, content, and emotions.

I met other people who were experiencing the same shift in awareness and peace of mind. They were particularly focused more on the now than the past or the future. They were drawing fewer lines between themselves and people who thought differently, recognizing that we are all human beings and that ultimately, we have to work together because there is nowhere else to go. Privately they shared with me that they were sensing an intervention from a higher authority, maybe from another dimension. They also said it didn't matter, that it was only what they knew and what came to their minds that would guide them.

33 - *Bits & Pieces*

Don't let yesterday use up too much of today. – Will Rogers

Mind Control - I realized one morning on a walk alone that I was in complete control of my being annoyed by someone in my life whom I otherwise cared about. I was in control because while I couldn't change her behavior, I could change my behavior and not to be annoyed by it. Yes, easier said than done, but awareness of that option was the key first step. It doesn't take as much energy to make that choice as it does to get riled up in annoyance and then come down from it, with an apology.

This underscores a critical option ... that you have control of your Ego. This is because you created the Ego and it is inside you. You can diminish the role of your Ego, and edit its responses to the people, places, and things that you encounter. The more you are award of this ability, the more you can practice it, the more your Ego will be reformed to better match your True Self.

Time Is on My Side - Most of my professional efforts since leaving ABC in New York for Mill Valley in 1980 have been freelance, meaning that I have not been working all the time, and most of my efforts have been offsite. I've worked mostly at home, and not on a M-F/9to5 schedule. (That said, I have never missed a deadline.)

More interesting is that over the last couple of years, I've made two interesting discoveries about time. One is that when I'm into my writing or editing - work that I enjoy - I've noticed that time seems to slow down. I don't look at the clock as often, and when I do, it's not as late as I expect it to be. For instance, it might be 9:30 instead of 10:30.

The second is more curious. Most days have a particular feel to them, and more frequently I'm noticing that they are not the right day. For instance, Sunday has always felt like a quieter sort of day. But sometimes the day will feel like a Sunday but in fact it is not. Maybe it's Tuesday. Or one morning, I was thinking of bringing the trash cans down to the road because the trucks come on Friday, until I realized that it was Monday.

There's no pattern to it; it's not every day or any number of days a week. Also, it's not in any way disturbing. It's just a curiosity. I mean, I know that certain things happen on certain days, but why should there be a feeling to them?

Facts Matter - A necessary factor of character and consciousness is truth. Character is soul deep. So is truth. Not partial truth, but the whole truth, and nothing but the truth. Well, you don't have to go overboard and say, "That new dress looks very good on you," when it doesn't, or the rock-hard asparagus was perfectly cooked. But you can appreciate the distinction. I don't know that this from Daniel Patrick Moynihan will clean up any uncertainty about what is the truth, but he made a significant point when he said, "You're entitled to your own opinion, but not to your own facts."

On Track - Important information comes to mind when (1) you are open and (2) you are on the right track. And getting on a track is easier than getting off it.

This note about what is easy. I was three days into a complicated video editing session, and after a big sigh, I said to my editor, "This sure ain't easy."

In the edit suite with us was the fellow who had done the sound recording for the shoot that we were editing. The soundman was one of the quietest people I'd ever worked with; he rarely said anything. He hadn't said a word to us in the past three days. The silence was broken when he said these words I'll never forget. He said, "If it was easy, anyone could do it."

Ideas Won't Keep - It's wonderful to have stimulating thoughts, but as Alfred North Whitehead counseled, "Ideas won't keep. Something must be done about them." In that vein there is considerable importance in writing down those thoughts. For they are just moments in your mind and can be forgotten ... genius lost forever. But writing them down deepens your hold of them because (1) your brain is dictating to your fingers to make the words on paper or on your digital screen, and (2) your eyes are seeing those words written. This is why diaries and journals can be valuable, for your personal and your professional life. I never leave my house without a notebook and two pens. (I find writing something down is more meaningful, perhaps because it requires more tactility.)

Old Soul - A friend of mine was in a bakery when a young woman came in pushing a carriage with an infant in it. My friend looked at the baby, and with a big smile said to him, "Oh, you are an old soul come back, aren't you?" The baby responded bright-eyed and gurgling gleefully. The mother freaked out and fled out the door with the baby in the carriage.

Energy Email - It was some time ago that I noticed it for the first time. It has happened a few times since, but with no pattern. I got an email from an old friend. It was just a half-dozen sentences, newsy but nothing ostensibly significant. However, my sense of my friend's feelings when he wrote the email was that he was in distress, even though there was nothing in the words themselves that indicated such a feeling. Still, just looking at the email as an image gave me the feeling that something was amiss.

I sent him a note that was a chatty response to what he had written, and then asked if everything was all right in his life. The next day he sent me an email that reported that his wife was ill. I sent my regards, of course, wishing her a full recovery. A few weeks later he sent a short note that thanked me for my good wishes and reporting that his wife was doing better.

He never said anything about why I had asked if he was all right. In fact, I never heard from him or about the matter again.

I think that somehow a person's emotions can be expressed in an otherwise staid email, but I don't know how. It probably happens more times that we realize, whatever is going on, but of course it wouldn't be noticed if the text mentioned something was wrong.

Our Perceptions - Figuring out the nature of the real world has obsessed scientists and philosophers for millennia. Three hundred years ago, the brilliant

Irish empiricist George Berkeley contributed a particularly prescient observation: The only thing we can perceive are our perceptions. In other words, consciousness is the matrix upon which the cosmos is apprehended. Color, sound, temperature, and the like exist only as perceptions in our head, not as absolute essences. In the broadest sense, we cannot be sure of an outside universe at all. What Berkeley observed was that each of us has our own, unique universe.

Blue Skies - As a private pilot of small planes, I pay serious attention to the quality of the fuel in the wing tanks to make sure there is no water in it. I don't want the engine to operate on anything but pure fuel. Similarly, we should think of our body as a temple, as the saying goes, and only put in it what will enable us to fly right.

When I looked up what were the best foods for a healthy mind, I could only find best foods for the brain. I suppose that somewhat makes sense since the brain is physical while the mind is energy. Anyway, here are some recommended foods to boost your brain and memory: fatty fish, coffee, blueberries, turmeric, broccoli, pumpkin seeds, dark chocolate, nuts, oranges, eggs, and green tea.

What a Strange Day - There were two significant

events as I was nearing the end of my walk. I was walking in the road to keep my distance from others. There was little traffic, and this was May of 2021 with the coronavirus still a threat, even though I had had my second vaccination.

I was about ten yards from the sidewalk when I heard the words "Tony Seton" spoken as though someone was calling my name, not loudly but to get my attention. I looked all around but saw no one near me. I didn't recognize the voice, nor did I hear it again after that. A few moments later I approached the curb.

On the sidewalk I saw a young woman, maybe 22-ish, in a state of distress. Such that when I asked her if she was all right, she started crying. I asked her if there was anything I could do. She shook her head, but clearly was gratified that someone cared enough to give her attention.

Gently but firmly I told her that she was going to feel better. She nodded. I said, "No really. I'm writing a book for people like you." She showed surprise and her face lightened. I said, "It doesn't matter about the future or the past. What matters is right now. Where you are living is in the present. It is already getting better."

She clearly rose out of her despair. And with that I smiled at her and walked away.

Intuition and Instinct - What are your most powerful senses? Smell, taste, touch, sight, hearing? No, they are intuition and instinct, the "non-senses" that know sooner than the tactile senses. They also get through to you through the hard senses.

Intuition is the ability to understand something immediately, without the need for conscious reasoning. Think about intuition. The word alone is a clue. *In-tuition.* Intuition is learning from what we know inside. It supersedes what thoughts are in your mind.

The word instinct is derivative from the Latin *instinguere* which means to prick, as to get attention, inside. The role of instinct is to override your thoughts to get your attention, and that's what feelings do.

The source of intuition and instinct is the True Self, and the True Self is in alignment with the larger reality. Whatever messaging you get from your True Self - specifically intuitive and instinctual - should grab your full attention immediately, especially if you have been thinking through your Ego.

Fine Fiction - I have heard people declare that they do not read fiction, and they say it in a superior tone. Such critics are missing a great trip. Fiction is not automatically throw-away useless. Some of the greatest writers ever were heralded for their fictional work. Writers like William Shakespeare, Mark

Twain, and Robertson Davies produced some of the finest literature ever. Just think of *The Merchant of Venice, Adventures of Huckleberry Finn,* and *What's Bred in the Bone.*

Fiction can describe people, places, and things in wonderful and vivid detail. It produces an important understanding of thoughts and feelings, illuminating conflicting positions, adding clarifying detail to a sketchy outline ... and does it in an entertaining style. It's like the difference between a five-star entertainment film and a slow documentary. As McLuhan noted, "Anyone who tries to make a distinction between education and entertainment doesn't know the first thing about either."

I love writing fiction. I find that it can be very instructive. In fact, I sometimes learn from what for my characters say - truly- and not infrequently words appear on the screen that didn't first visit my cognitive mind. More on that in Chapter 21 - Creativity.

For the record, this book is <u>not</u> a work of fiction. I'm a veteran journalist, and everything I've written in these pages has been the product of my own investigation and reasoned surmise.

34 - Thoughts of Sri Mokki

I have hardly ever known a mathematician who was capable of reasoning. – Plato

- We define ourselves as human beings in one way ... by what thoughts we select and how we process them. Your mind is literally the center of everything. You decide what thoughts to perceive. All the thoughts of the past and the future are there for your mind to entertain.

- We can hardly entertain new thoughts if our mind is filled with old ones. When we take old thoughts out of the way, we make room in our mind for more, new, and fresh. If you could stop thinking, if you stopped filling your mind from morning 'til night, you might realize how you are consuming yourself with unimportance.

- Holding onto a thought is like you are on a river and you tie up your boat to a place on the shore. It may be beautiful, but why stop? You hold yourself to the past. There is much more, beyond your imagination, that awaits you.

- You cannot not think. Your mind will always seize on something. Nature abhors a vacuum.

- Life is about creating. The real practice is to keep your mind clear in your everyday life. To be constantly available to the flow of thoughts that are the universe. To dip your bucket into that flow, empty it, and refill it. In every moment.

- You will have many thoughts recur, but only until they are resolved. This is because as you empty your mind of deliberation, you expand the vocabulary of your consciousness. With this wider range of contemplative values, you will be able to consider certain ideas more effectively. Just as a child won't appreciate the depth of Shakespeare's sonnets as will an adult. You do not have to retrieve thoughts. If they need to be considered, they will return to your consciousness unbidden.

- Planning is coming to decisions early. And by definition, without as much information as we might have by waiting to make the decision at the time it needed to be made. This doesn't mean no planning at all. We live in this temporal world which requires some thought. We plant gardens to raise food. We put fuel in the car to travel long distances. But too often, we think and think and think about matters that either cannot be resolved in that moment or should better be managed spontaneously.

- We have judgments because society insists that we position ourselves by condemning those who aren't part of our society. An extreme example. You are walking toward a man and suddenly he takes out a gun and fires shots all around you. You do not have good feelings for this man. But then you turn around and see that you were about to be attacked, and this man has killed your attackers. Your first judgment was one of anger and fear. Your revised judgment is one of relief and gratitude. Completely contradictory. Judgments hold you back. They are decisions from the past. They block your view of the present. Releasing a judgment frees you to have an open mind and an accurate contemporary assessment of a person or a situation that might benefit from a free look.

- It is important to understand the difference between thoughts and feelings. Thoughts and feelings come from the same place - from the source of all things; Nature, the Universe, The Force - and they are received by your soul ... your True Self. A key difference between thoughts and feelings, is that thoughts are intuited and arrive in the mind where

they might be interpreted by your Ego and so therein can be colored by your disposition. Feelings seize your being through instinct. When they are felt cleanly, they are interpreted truthfully, but if your Ego doesn't want to experience the feeling, it can be deliberately misread.
But feelings can be very powerful. They can overwhelm your thoughts, at least temporarily. By the same token, you can have thoughts that can instigate feelings.
It's all in your control. And that's the key. You decide how you will receive thoughts and feelings, in what context you will frame them, and how you will have them affect you.

- Regarding meditation, if it is helpful for you, go for it. But looking in from the outside, what sense does it make to sit in a darkened room, twisted up like a pretzel, focusing on your breathing? Your mind will not be emptied into nothing. Why not instead go for a walk in the woods or by the river? Most humans are better served by allowing their soul to fill with Nature's sights and sounds and smells. After all, Nature is your source, the source of all. It is more natural to see the flowers or hear the owl, than it is to try to empty your mind.

-Visualization is another popular exercise. Especially for those who want to feed a hope or hope to influence their future. But there is an inherent flaw in such thinking, which is that people are likely to visualize an outcome that is not best for them. Indeed, reality might be better than what they are hoping for. And by focusing on their visualized hope, they may walk right past the better path.

- We can better know people if we receive them based on their energy rather than on what our eyes take in.

- In normal discourse, you shouldn't have to think before you speak. Like an athlete swinging a bat or throwing a ball, his calculations are out of sight. When you think first, you put your Ego - cognitive thoughts - before your higher mind. Just speak.

- Don't explain what is known. If the person to whom you are talking doesn't understand something you are saying, surely he will make that clear.

- The less you struggle to hold on to what you think you know, the more you learn, the better you understand, and the closer you engage what Ferlinghetti called "the rebirth of wonder." It takes a lot to reach an understanding of - and then practice - experiencing life as effortless, but when you tap into it, you will discover that you will be less engaged and more entertained.

Appendix

Wendy Palmer is the founder of Leadership Embodiment, a process that uses principles from the non-violent Japanese martial art of Aikido and mindfulness to offer simple tools and practices to increase leadership capacity and respond to stress and pressure with greater confidence and integrity. Wendy holds a seventh-degree black belt in Aikido and has practiced mindfulness for over 40 years.

She has worked with executive teams and individuals for Twitter, Genentech, Capital One, Jazz Pharmaceuticals, The Gap, NASA, Salesforce, McKinsey & Co, Oracle, Unilever, The BBC, Gates Foundation, The George Washington University, Comcast, Accenture, BlackRock Funds, and The Daimler Chrysler Group. She is also an author of four books, *Dragons and Power, Leadership Embodiment, The Intuitive Body,* and *The Practice of Freedom.*

More about Wendy at
https://leadershipembodiment.com/

4 Ways to Tap Into the Collective Unconscious for Inspiration

Collective unconscious can give us immense creative breakthroughs. Many famous authors have claimed that they have written some of their best work as if possessed, dictated, unconscious!

* * * * *

The great fiction writer George Eliot said that in all of her best writings, something that was "not herself" took possession of her; that the words she wrote felt as if they came from this "other personality".

The poet John Keats wrote that sections of his famous work, Hyperion, came to him "by chance or magic - to be, as it were, something given to me." He added that he had not been "aware of the beauty of some thought or expression until after I'd composed and written it down."

The German polymath Goethe wrote of his famous novel, *The Sorrows of Young Werther,* "I wrote the book almost unconsciously, like a somnambulist, and was amazed when I realized what I had done."

William Blake, the famous English poet and painter, said of his work *Milton,* "I have written this poem from immediate dictation, twelve or sometimes twenty or thirty lines at a time, without premeditation, and even against my will."

Robert Louis Stevenson, author of *Dr. Jekyll and Mr. Hyde,* wrote about the existence of little helpers from his unconscious, "who do one half my work while I am fast asleep, and in all human likelihood, do the rest for me as well, when I am wide awake and fondly suppose I do it for myself."

"My brain is only a receiver, in the Universe, there is a core from which we obtain knowledge, strength, and inspiration. I have not penetrated into the secrets of this core, but I know that it exists." Nikola Tesla

"I wrote the book almost unconsciously, like a somnambulist, and was amazed when I realized what I had done." Goethe on The Sorrows of Young Werther

(https://medium.com/inspirationwise/4-ways-to-tap-into-the-collective-unconscious-for-inspiration-8e055b7e9e06)

In and of the World

To give credit where it is certainly due for this delicious film and excellent script, please note that the brilliant Billy Wilder directed *Sabrina* and co-wrote the screenplay with Ernest Lehman and Samuel A. Taylor who wrote the book, *Sabrina Fair.* In the film, Audrey Hepburn played Sabrina Fairchild.

https://www.imdb.com/title/tt0047437/characters/nm0000030

The Ultimate App

About the Author

Tony Seton is a journalist, writer, publisher, public speaker, business/political consultant, and communications specialist. As an award-winning broadcast journalist for ABC TV, he covered Watergate, six elections, and five space shots. And he produced Barbara Walters' news interviews, and business/economics coverage.

Later, he wrote and produced two award-winning public television documentaries. He has conducted over 2,600 interviews, and is the author of more than 2,300 essays.

Through Seton Publishing, Tony has edited and published more than 40 of his own books and screenplays, and 30+ for clients.

As a political consultant, his clients have included Nancy Pelosi, Tom Campbell, the American Nurses Association, and a plethora of local candidates.

He has taught journalism and writing, provided media training, and produced websites.

Tony is also a private pilot and a photographer.

SETON
PUBLISHING

Made in the USA
Middletown, DE
18 September 2022

10550980R00097